Hans Günther Meissner

Strategic International Marketing

With 44 Figures and 33 Tables

Springer-Verlag
Berlin Heidelberg New York
London Paris Tokyo
Hong Kong

Professor Dr. Hans Günther Meissner
Lehrstuhl für Marketing
Universität Dortmund
Postfach 500 500
D-4600 Dortmund 50, FRG

ISBN-13:978-3-642-75479-1 e-ISBN-13:978-3-642-75477-7
DOI: 10.1007/978-3-642-75477-7

Library of Congress Cataloging-in-Publication Data
Meissner, Hans Günther.
[Strategisches internationales Marketing. English]
Strategic international marketing / Hans Günther Meissner.
p. cm.
Translation of: Strategisches internationales Marketing.
Includes bibliographical references.
ISBN-13:978-3-642-75479-1 (U.S.)
1. Export marketing--Germany (West)
2. Foreign trade promotion--Germany (West)
3. Export marketing. I. Title.
HF 1009.7.G3M4513 1990
382'.6'0943--dc20

Softcover reprint of the hardcover 1st edition 1990

2142/7130-543210

Foreword

The growing dynamic of the world economy is exerting an increasing influence on the economy and the economic development of many countries and many companies. The international division of labour has become a key factor in economic development. The commercial success of many companies is determined both by international possibilities of sales and purchase, and also by international alternatives of finance and production.

The importance of internationalisation and its significance for company policy first made themselves felt with the multinational and international companies and contributed to the world success of individual companies. However, with increasing export quotas and with the differentiation of foreign activities, internationalisation is growing in significance for those companies which have previously only been nationally oriented, and consequently, for firms of medium size.

The internationalisation of the activities of companies is influenced in a far-reaching manner by the field factors which companies have to take into account on a variety of foreign markets. Here, in addition to legal and economic field factors, one is dealing in particular with sociocultural constraints which the companies can influence either not at all or only to a very limited extent, so that they must adjust themselves to these constraints in a differentiated manner. The companies thus find themselves confronted by a strategic choice between a world-wide unification of production and marketing programmes, and internationally differentiated programmes sensitively attuned to the national and regional particularities of the individual sub-markets. The necessity and the opportunity of internationalisation require of the companies an intensified strategic orientation, that is, one which is long-term and comprehensive. Dependence on development in a variety of foreign markets makes it necessary to consider, for example, within the context of a strategic overall concept, the varying rates of inflation in the individual countries, the flexibility of exchange rates and any commercial, economic and political changes. In addition to this, the companies must adjust themselves to the interrelationship between the world economy and world politics. Worldwide global orientation requires companies to follow a worldwide global strategic concept. For many companies this means stepping onto a whole new continent in company policy. To take these steps, the companies must undergo far-reaching learning processes.

This development towards the internationalisation of company activities coincides with the basic marketing orientation of companies which has been created in the context of the rise of buyers' markets and market saturations in important market segments in the majority of the industrial countries. Also, companies can no longer bring technological innovations onto the market without considering anything but technical aspects, but must support them above all by appropriate marketing.

The reality of company management is today indelibly marked by these twin developments towards internationalisation and towards marketing. The consequence for companies is to be found therefore in an appropriate and consistent orientation towards **Strategic International Marketing**.

This book concerns itself with marking out the perspectives and possibilities as well as the instruments of Strategic International Marketing, as these have emerged in the course of recent developments. The central aspect is the integration of marketing considerations with internationalisation strategies. The perspective of the book is directed towards the situation of German companies. However, the experiences of companies in other countries, especially in the EC, the USA and Japan are also considered in this book.

An important basis of the book was provided by conversations and interviews which I conducted with a variety of leading executives of international companies, to whom I am greatly indebted. I am also grateful for the stimulation and the encouragement which I received from the members of the European International Business Association (EIBA).

My especial thanks are due to my colleagues in the Department of Marketing at the University of Dortmund, who have supported me in a multitude of ways in the writing of this book;

thus I wish to thank Dr. Thomas E. Banning for his constructive co-operation and Mr. Ernst J. Baumann, especially for preparing the publication of this edition. The English version of this book was realised by Mr. Noel Deeney, College of Marketing & Design, Dublin/Ireland, who did the difficult translation of the German version in a professional and highly sensible way.

Dortmund, Mai 1990 HANS GUENTHER MEISSNER

Contents

A. Developments towards Strategic International Marketing

1. Growth: Target-Setting and the Development of Companies

Ever since the Industrial Revolution, the development of the world economy, in conjunction with technological progress, has forced business enterprises into a never-ceasing and frequently decisive process of growth. This compulsion towards growth affects not just long-established companies; for example, newly-created ones in the high-tech area come to experience it very quickly.

This historical drive towards growth, which is characteristic of industrial development in all parts of the world, is particularly connected with the increasing pressure of fixed costs on the decision processes of companies. The higher the proportion of fixed costs, the greater the product output of the companies must become in order to remain internationally competitive. The profitability and the market position of companies, and thus their power to innovate and expand, depend decisively on the possibilities of mass production and on the utilisation of learning curves.

The safeguarding of profitability on the one hand and the build-up of market position on the other condition in their turn the innovative ability of companies. The safeguarding of the existence of companies depends, in the long-term, on their ability to develop new products and processes appropriate to the market.[1] Market position, profitability and innovative ability thus all stand in a systematic interrelationship, to which Porter[2] in particular has drawn attention, and which has not previously been analysed with sufficient precision in traditional German business management theory.

This situation has led to two different strategic consequences for companies: to the orientation towards Strategic Marketing, and towards International Marketing.

---

[1] Cf. Meissner, H. G., Marketing für Innovationen, in: Meissner, H. G., Winkelgrund, R. (Eds.), Marketing für Innovationen, Dortmund 1984, pp. 9–22, here p. 14.

[2] Cf. Porter, M. E., Competitive Strategy, Techniques for analyzing industries and competitors, New York 1980.

The development towards **Strategic Marketing** has been stimulated particularly by the process of increasing market saturation in many areas of the consumer goods spectrum, which has shown itself to be an effective brake on growth. In stagnating or in shrinking markets, the necessary orientation towards growth cannot in the long-run be attained solely by tactical or operational marketing activities, such as advertising campaigns or price reductions. The marketing concept of companies thus requires a much more long-term orientation and at the same time the sensitive consideration of the dynamics of the environmental factors, which express themselves in changes in the political and legal framework, in a change of values among consumers or in technological change.[3] The orientation of company policy towards the environment forces companies to develop a new and appropriate company culture. Authoritative claims to leadership made by companies on the basis of their engineering achievements, and subject to these, can no longer guarantee lasting success on the marketplace; much more relevant to this is a high level of sensitization towards the environment in which the companies are active.[4] In this area, an energetic and profound process of change in the self-understanding and in the market orientation of companies is now under way.

The orientation towards **International Marketing** is closely connected with this process of change in business and in company management. After the Second World War and the reconstruction of German industry, nationalisation measures and technical advance led in many branches to a situation where the capacities built up proved to be too large for the internal market. For the companies concerned this led to the necessity of overcoming the limitations of the national borders and of realising additional sales outlets, especially through exports to a variety of foreign markets.[5]

The German companies thus followed a strategy of internationalisation, such as was already typical for smaller countries like the Netherlands and Switzerland. This situation is not so clearly marked with companies which can rely on large internal markets. It is only recently that the American economy has been confronted with a similar situation and is now, under the pressure of

---

[3] For a discussion of developments in the environment which are of significance for strategic decisions, see for example Meffert, H., Perspektiven des Marketing in den 80er Jahren, in Meffert, H. (Ed.), Marketing im Wandel, Wiesbaden 1980, pp. 3–35; Raffée, H., Marketing-Perspektiven der 80er Jahre, in: Marketing, Vol. 4, No. 2, pp. 1–16; Tietz, B., Die Wertedynamik der Konsumenten und Unternehmer in ihren Konsequenzen auf das Marketing, in: Marketing, Vol. 4, No. 2, pp. 91–102.

[4] Cf. Raffée, H., Grundlagen und Ansätze des strategischen Marketing, in: Raffée, H., Wiedermann, K.-P. (Eds.), Strategisches Marketing, Stuttgart 1985, pp. 5–9.

[5] See on this point for example Meissner, H. G., Exportpolitik vom Standpunkt der Unternehmensführung, Herne and Berlin 1974; Ringle, G., Exportmarketing, Wiesbaden 1977; Dichtl, E., Issing, O. (Eds.), Exporte als Herausforderung für die deutsche Wirtschaft, Cologne 1984.

imports from Europe and Asia, making increasing efforts to open up foreign sales markets. German companies learned from their experience seeking outlets on foreign markets that their market success depends on the most precise alignment possible to the international environment. The observance of foreign legal norms and commercial practices, the consideration of cultural particularities and the mastering of foreign languages are important prerequisites for long-term success on foreign markets. In International Marketing, company culture thus underwent a process of adjustment and alteration, parallel to the turn towards Strategic Marketing.

The orientation of companies towards Strategic Marketing and International Marketing has in the case of German companies up to the present hardly occurred in any integrated manner. In practice, International Marketing was developed from traditional export efforts, without creating sufficient links to the total situation of the company. In addition to this, however, International Marketing has to deal to an ever-increasing extent with the other possible foreign activities in the form of direct foreign investments, franchises and cooperative agreements, which have to be made because of financial, company-strategic and legal considerations. Strategic Marketing has been driven forward by planning and development departments, and particularly in connection with the forcing-through of technological innovations. With the further technical and commercial development of companies and against a backdrop of the dynamics of the world economy, the necessity of integrating these two lines of orientation and guidance into a unitary policy for companies makes itself ever more clearly felt.

The consequence for companies therefore consists in the urgent creation of a policy of **Strategic International Marketing**.

The integration to Strategic International Marketing (Diagram 1) follows in principle the suggestions developed by Ansoff, which may be presented in a nine-field matrix. (Table 1).

Diagram 1. Integration to Strategic International Marketing

Table 1. Product-market matrix in International Marketing

Products / Markets	Traditional Products	Altered Products	New Products
Home Market			
Traditional Export Markets			
New Foreign Markets			

In the strategic concept of companies, a position of great importance is assigned to the selection and the cultivation of foreign markets. In Strategic International Marketing therefore, particular emphasis is placed on the informational prerequisites and on the decision-making criteria for the selection and opening-up of international markets.

On the one hand, companies must react to the international environment, e.g. by the offer of specific problem solutions in the area of investment goods, and on the other hand they must place their own formative stamp on the international environment, as has been the case for example with the Eastern Bloc Committee of German Industry in their dealings with the countries of state trade. For the implementation of Strategic International Marketing, it has on many occasions become evident that the order of the national state is too narrow for considerations of commercial necessity and of the opportunities for company development. For this reason, the realisation of the European Community is to be considered a major step in extending the strategic framework of the action of companies. This is made clear not least by the figures relating to the development of foreign trade within the Community. At the same time it becomes obvious that a distinct political element must be brought into the strategic decision horizon of companies, since market development on many foreign markets is dependent on internal as well as on external political constellations. Traditional business management theory treats such political factors, insofar as it mentions them at all, solely as environmental conditions, and not as necessary decision parameters for the strategic target-setting of companies.

The structure of opportunity and risk for companies which are internationally active is influenced by a whole series of external factors, which are considered within the framework of Strategic International Marketing. The essential factors of external influence, which must be included within the strategic concept of companies are especially:

- the overall development of world trade,
- economic development on individual foreign markets,
- the sociocultural environmental conditions in individual foreign markets or groups of countries and
- the political and legal environmental conditions.

2. World Economic Developments and World Politics

The division of labour in the world economy has in the course of recent years and decades reached a level never previously attained in the course of economic history. International trade is no longer just the exception within nationally oriented economic systems and is not restricted to a few specialised companies, but is well on the way to becoming the dominant dynamic factor not just in the economic, but also in the political, social and cultural development of the world. This quantitatively measurable process has opened a new qualitative dimension to world trade and the world economy and thereby also to world politics.

The process of world economic integration did not run evenly and without interruption, but led again and again to tensions and conflicts, whether about raw materials and conditions of supply or about national competitive advantages. At present, such tensions exhibit themselves particularly in the international debts of most developing and state trade countries. Related to this is the factor of disturbance inherent in the chronic trade and balance of payments deficits of some countries and the corresponding persistent surpluses of others. This imbalance is also a burden at the present time to the international exchange relationship between the USA and Japan. The developments which become manifest in such surpluses and deficits are simultaneously an expression of structurally conditioned imbalances in the development of the world economy. The attempt to dismantle the existing imbalances by one-sided protectionist measures presents in this situation a specific risk within the politics of trade, to the maintenance and above all to the further development of the international division of labour.

The processes of integration to larger economic units, to free trade zones or economic communities, play a central role in world economic development. In this context, the European Community has attained a crucial significance for the foreign trade of West Germany, and also for the economies of the other member states. With the entry of Spain and Portugal at the beginning of 1986, the market of the European Community grew to one of 322 million potential customers. Foreign business deals within the European Community are now scarcely regarded by companies as foreign trade in the classic sense, but have achieved a special status as Community trade. The existence of the European Community has, in addition to reducing formal trade barriers, also noticeably and effectively diminished the psychological distance among the individual countries.

Because of its lesser integrative power, the European Free Trade Association has not achieved that level of trade-creating effectiveness which the EC has managed to realise for its member countries. The integrative power of the Council for Mutual Economic Aid (COMECON) is clearly determined by formative political intentions within the state trade countries and is especially influenced by the leadership role assumed by the Soviet Union. Attempts to form comparable economic unions in other countries of the world, e.g. in Africa, Asia or Latin America, have not been able to achieve the level of economic success which has been realised in the European Community.

The international world economic network is at present concentrated on the European Community, the USA and Japan. There has arisen here a **triad** of world economic interrelationships,[6] which has become the dominant dynamic factor of the world economy and of world politics.

The dynamic of the world economy cannot be separated from developments and trends in world politics. The great fields of tension in world politics also affect the world economy. Significant ones at present from a European point of view are:

- the East-West conflict,
- the North-South divide,
- the South Africa conflict and
- the Middle East conflict.

In addition to these, there is a multitude of areas of tension and crisis which do not, it is true, affect the totality of world economic development, but do indeed influence economic relations with individual regions. One might name here for example, the former war between Iran and Iraq, the Nicaraguan conflict or the internal political tensions in Sri Lanka. Furthermore, recent decades have seen the rise of regional consciousness among, for example, the Basques and the Northern Irish, the Kurds and the Chinese minorities in Indonesia and Malaysia, which all has an inhibiting effect on any further extension of world economic relationships. All these focus-points of conflict represent actual and potential disruptive factors for the further development of the world economy. In the decision processes of companies they emerge as political risks.

---

[6] Cf. Ohmae, Kenichi, Die Macht der Triade, Wiesbaden 1985.

The awareness of the unity of the world and the world economy is today much stronger among companies than among many politicians. The latter are not infrequently concerned with borders and with questions of national sovereignty, whereas companies must, as a matter of their own self-interest, turn their attention towards the lessening of tensions and the dismantling of borders. The reality of today's world economic network makes companies tend towards a global viewpoint and interest themselves much more strongly in the unity of the world and its further economic development and therefore also its simultaneous political and social development, than is the case with many politicians, who frequently still pursue the anachronistic and now meaningless conflict patterns of the pre-industrial or early industrial period. There thus arises a new type of field of tension between companies and politics.

In the context of the conflict potential in the world economy, the discussion concerning a new world economic order plays a central role. A number of developing countries is trying to have a new world economic order adopted at international level, which fundamentally improves the position of these countries in the world economy and dismantles the structural advantages of the established industrial countries. This demand for a new "just" world economic order ignores, however, certain fundamental interrelationships of the world economy. It is not least the high living standard of the industrial countries which enables them to offer market opportunities to the developing countries, and the economic growth of the industrial countries has a price-raising effect on the market situation of important industrial raw materials, so that the developing and threshold countries receive high incomes which they in turn urgently require for the necessary processes of their further industrialisation, urbanisation and rationalisation. Even the requisite transfer of technological know-how can only take place if the developing countries are prepared to recognise the corresponding property rights.

Quite independently of ideological positions adopted by some politicians, various journalists and individual academics, the world economy today is determined by a broadly **partner-based system** of foreign trade, which has replaced both the traditional colonial and the imperial patterns of foreign trade. This partner-based foreign trade is a consequence of the actually existing union of all countries of the world. The more intense the world economic networking of companies, countries and economic communities becomes, the greater grows the interest in having the other countries as potential customers, suppliers or even as good debtors. This wish is linked to an interest in having a world which is as free as possible from conflict and in which a liberal economic order prevails. The concept that one country could draw advantages from foreign trade, one-sidedly and at the cost of other countries, has its roots in the colonial or imperial world of ideas. Communication and information have forged the world economy into a factual unity, whose ability to function is in the interest of all countries and all companies and organisations, and which also frequently transcends the ideological barriers in the world.

The interest in a new world economic order should therefore direct its attention towards the dismantling of barriers, artificial export subventions and exchange rates which are either manipulated for political reasons or distorted for speculative ones. The functional capability of the world economy has today become the decisive factor for the growth and the international activity of companies in many countries of the world. This is particularly true for the companies of the triad.

3. The Internationalisation of Business Management Theory

The increasing interconnectedness of all aspects of the world economy and the growing proportion of foreign activities among companies lead to a situation where business management theory must concern itself to a greater extent with the international processes of information, decision and formation. The necessity of this is further emphasised by the existence of firms which are active multinationally.[7] As in some other countries, this development has led in the USA to the creation of a special subject within the business management curriculum, **"International Management"** or **"International Business"**.

German business management theory has up to the present closed its doors against the admission of a special subject which concentrates on international management problems. Instead of this, approval is given to the addition of an international dimension to individual teaching or research areas which are institutionally or functionally limited, without there being, however, any noticeable development in this regard so far. There thus arises the danger that German business management theory is distancing itself from the actual and concrete problems with which companies are confronted.

Against a background of the historical development of business management theory, which has unfolded in close connection with the prevailing problems of companies, it becomes clear that the further development of this science can only proceed via an orientation towards the problems of practice and through close co-operation between academics and companies. The structure of business management research and teaching in West Germany is, however, only partially oriented towards such co-operation, so that it is

[7] See on this point e.g. the contributions in: Kebschull, D., Mayer, O. G.(Eds.), Multinationale Unternehmen – Anfang oder Ende der Weltwirtschaft, Frankfurt/M. 1974.

precisely in the area of international company management that a noticeable gap has appeared between the problems and commercial necessities of companies on the one hand, and the areas of research and the teaching syllabi of business management theory on the other.

The necessity for a systematic coming to terms with the problems of international production, finance, organisation and sales becomes all the greater as international business climbs as a proportion of the overall turnover of companies. This necessity comes particularly to the fore when it is a matter of the structure-shaping, strategic decisions of the companies, on which the future existence of these companies will depend.

In this context of long-term and international company decisions, the significance of Strategic International Marketing becomes evident. Decisions in international markets represent a major category of strategic decisions which is now of growing importance for West German companies and will become even more so in the future.

The internationalisation of business management theory requires primarily an intensification of research in the area of International Strategic Marketing. Internationally oriented business management theory overlaps to a considerable thematic extent with International Marketing. For it is above all the expansion of the possibilities of sales and purchase which stimulates companies to build up their international activities, so that marketing research has given rise to a variety of impulses for the internationalisation of business management theory. Despite this significance of marketing, however, one must recognise that the further development to International Business Management Theory will only be made possible by the foundation of an autonomous area of research which is independent of the interests which any of the individual disciplines within business management theory might have in international matters.

The internationalisation of business management theory requires, rather, a synergistic approach, in order to be able to integrate the various aspects which range from international financing, via the various forms of foreign investment, the international exchange of patents and licences or the drawing-up of world balances of trade, right up to International Marketing.

This integration requires a new, creative and holistic concept, which either cannot be achieved or at best can be achieved only in discrete packages by means of the traditional analytical processes of business management theory, split as they are across various spheres of research. It must aim not just at overcoming fragmentation into different areas of management research, but must also take relevant findings of related disciplines into account. Thus, it is a matter of the utmost necessity to consider not just economic but also behavioural and legal theoretical concepts in order to develop a consistent theory of international company management which is directed towards the trading requirements of companies. It is precisely within the international environment of companies that the particularities of human behaviour have to be regarded. The problem field of international management underlines the necessity for business management to open itself across a broad front to the methods and insights of the behavioural sciences. International Business Management Theory, and therefore also Strategic International Marketing, can only be created with the aid of an interdisciplinary concept.

B. The Dynamics of the World Economy

1. The International Division of Labour and the Extent of World Trade

The present level of the international division of labour makes itself evident to a large number of companies in their high and still growing export quotas. This level and international trading relationships present companies with a previously unparalleled source of potential opportunity, but also with a new type of risk, since turnover and company success are now becoming in the most far-reaching manner dependent on political, economic and social developments in other countries of the world and especially on developments in the essential sales and purchase markets.

In recent years another aspect of the development of world trade has become increasingly evident: namely that the growth in world trade has always been greater than the growth of the world social product. Foreign trade has thus become the important motor of economic development in the world. Its dynamic has however also led to profound structural changes in the international competitiveness of individual countries, branches of industry and companies, so that traditional export markets cease or are lost to other producers. Yet on the other hand the activities of companies have opened up new international markets.

The analysis of the growth of the world economy and world trade, as well as of world economic changes and competitive processes is the prerequisite for companies to be able to adjust to the new type of situation. The following statistics of world exports and world imports make clear important structural and dynamic aspects of world trade. (Table 2). This evidence shows that world trade has increased its value sevenfold within the last 20 years.

Table 2. The development of world trade between 1967 and 1987[1]
Part 1: Imports

Year	World					Europe		Outside Europe	
	including state trade countries[1]	excluding state trade countries							
	Value		Index of Value[2]	Index of Average Value[3]	Index of Volume[3]	Value	Index of Value[2]	Value	Index of Value[2]
	Millions DM		1980 = 100			Millions DM	1980 =100	Millions DM	1980 =100
	Imports								
1967	901000	807200	24	25	43	401800	24	405400	24
1968	999520	898000	26	25	49	442240	26	455760	26
1969	1128540	1007920	30	25	54	510310	30	497610	29
1971	1274120	1141840	34	28	62	587400	35	554440	32
1972	1378500	1332500	36	30	68	640000	38	592500	34
1973	1575006	1411000	41	37	76	744300	44	666700	39
1974	2203600	2001000	59	53	79	996500	59	1004500	58
1975	2216400	1971400	58	58	73	971600	58	999800	58
1976	2549300	2289900	67	58	83	1126800	67	1163100	68
1977	2684100	2421400	71	64	87	1171200	70	1249000	72
1978	2696200	2425100	71	71	91	1179500	70	1245600	72
1979	3077000	2791000	83	83	99	1402000	83	1389000	81
1980	3737000	3403000	100	100	100	1680000	100	723000	100
1981	4589000	4166000	122	99	100	1850000	110	2316000	134
1982	4656000	4210000	124	94	99	1892000	113	2318000	135
1983	4810000	4319000	127	90	101	1905000	113	2414000	140
1984	5664000	5100000	150	88	109	2163000	129	2937000	170
1985	5960000	5312000	156	86	113	2337000	139	2975000	173
1986	4807000	4290000	126	88	122	2038000	121	2252000	131
1987	4590000	4145000	122	...	...	2061000	123	2084000	212

[1] Details for the state trade countries are partially estimates
[2] Calculated in DM
[3] Calculated in US$ (Adjustments 1975 = 100 for 1968 to 1972)

---

[1] Taken from Statistisches Bundesamt (Ed.), Statistisches Jahrbuch 1988 für die Bundesrepublik Deutschland, Stuttgart and Mainz 1988, p.689.

Part 2: Exports

Year	World					Europe		Outside Europe	
	including state trade countries[1]	excluding state trade countries							
	Value		Index of Value[2]	Index of Average Value[3]	Index of Volume[3]	Value	Index of Value[2]	Value	Index of Value[2]
	Millions DM		1980 = 100			Millions DM	1980 =100	Millions DM	1980 =100
	Exports								
1967	858760	759200	23	25	41	363640	25	395560	22
1968	957040	849200	26	25	47	406560	27	442640	24
1969	1077710	957050	29	26	52	468740	32	488310	27
1970	1144870	1020770	31	27	57	505100	34	515670	28
1971	1219780	1089800	33	28	61	546550	37	543250	30
1972	1336300	1197500	36	31	66	605400	41	592100	32
1973	1541100	1384100	42	36	79	690600	47	693500	38
1974	2176600	1987800	60	50	83	877500	59	1110300	61
1975	2146800	1936200	58	56	77	896200	61	1040000	57
1976	2491900	2258800	68	57	86	1013200	68	1245600	68
1977	2608500	2359500	71	62	90	1078000	73	1281500	70
1978	2613900	2364800	71	69	94	1129100	76	1234900	67
1979	3010000	2739000	83	82	100	1287500	87	1451500	79
1980	3628000	3313000	100	100	100	1480000	10	1833000	100
1981	4462000	4052000	122	99	100	1697000	115	2355000	128
1982	4497000	4034000	122	94	97	1762000	119	2272000	124
1983	4619000	4106000	124	89	100	1807000	122	2299000	125
1984	5420000	4843000	146	87	107	2077000	140	2766000	151
1985	5668000	5070000	153	86	111	2269000	153	2801000	153
1986	4591000	4103000	124	90	117	2039000	138	2064000	113
1987	4410000	3972000	120	...	...	2034000	137	1938000	106

[1] Details for the state trade countries are partially estimates
[2] Calculated in DM
[3] Calculated in US$ (Adjustments 1975 = 100 for 1968 to 1972)

Table 3. Imports and exports by country[2]
Part 1: Imports of the most important countries*

Country	1984	1985	1986	1987		1986	1987
	DM (Millions)				%	DM per inhabitant	
United States	972354	1063181	839967	763348	16.6	3427	3114
West Germany	434257	463811	413744	409641	8.9	6775	6697
France	295757	316309	277443	282998	6.2	5006	5106
United Kingdom	300220	320782	272224	276548	6.0	4779	4885
Japan	382633	374886	259149	268911	5.9	2133	2213
Italy	233693	259142	216511	224428	4.9	3783	3921
USSR	229778	242833	192852	182585	4.0	688	652
Canada	208706	223054	173245	157649	3.4	6765	6156
Netherlands	176898	191967	163861	163922	3.6	11254	11258
Belgium/Luxembourg	155000	163349	147614	149422	3.3	14373	14549
China[1]	72511	125371	93707	77760	1.7	87	73
Switzerland	83566	90059	89398	90738	2.0	13690	13896
Spain	81539	88204	76852	87899	9	1987	2273
Hong Kong	81415	86965	76745	87233	1.9	13878	15500
Sweden	75059	83751	70509	73082	1.6	8424	8731
South Korea	87299	91539	68537	73080	1.6	164	1758
Austria	55782	61475	58249	58639	1.3	7705	7756
Singapore	81827	77281	55360	58153	1.3	21375	22453
Australia	67320	69791	54726	...	...	3427	...
Taiwan	62583	59100	52437	62104	1.4	2709	3208
Totals	4138197	4452850	3653130	...	...	X	X
Other countries	1525803	1507150	1153870	...	...	X	X
World	5664000	5960000	4807000	4590000	100	X	X

* Arranged in order of the size of imports in 1986
[1] Without Taiwan

[2] Taken from Statistisches Bundesamt (Ed.), Statistisches Jahrbuch 1988 für die Bundesrepublik Deutschland, Stuttgart and Mainz 1988, p. 678.

Part 2: Exports of the most important countries*

Country	1984	1985	1986	1987		1986	1987
	DM (Millions)				%	DM per inhabitant	
West Germany	488223	537164	526363	527377	12.0	8620	8621
United States	620981	626650	471550	455159	10.3	1924	1857
Japan	484607	516248	453706	412610	9.4	3735	3396
France	265256	286522	258316	257128	5.8	4661	4640
United Kingdom	268860	297222	231438	234886	5.3	4063	4124
Italy	209071	231324	212259	208955	4.7	3708	3651
USSR	261199	256372	211218	204835	4.6	754	731
Canada	241073	251590	182862	169909	3.9	7140	6634
Netherlands	187604	200949	174721	166675	3.8	12000	11447
Belgium /Luxembourg	145258	156750	148968	149126	3.4	14505	14521
Taiwan	86801	90325	86343	96361	2.2	4460	4977
Switzerland	73050	80216	81581	81450	1.8	12493	12473
Sweden	83427	89257	80545	79902	1.8	9623	9546
Hong Kong	80706	88354	76905	87253	2.0	13907	15553
South Korea	83348	89032	75330	84780	1.9	1812	2039
China[1]	69066	80566	67363	71100	1.	6	66
Spain	66357	71346	59151	61162	1.4	1530	1582
Saudi Arabia	105089	80791	53764	...	...	4477	...
East Germany	65050	66652	53341	...	...	3209	...
Austria	44780	50629	48859	48755	1.1	6463	6449
Totals	3930806	4147959	3554583	...	...	X	X
Other countries	1489194	1520041	1036417	...	...	X	X
World	5420000	5668000	4591000	4410000	100	X	X

* Arranged in order of the size of exports in 1986
[1] Without Taiwan

The shares of the most important countries engaged in world trade may be seen from Table 3.

From the same Table, one may simultaneously see that, with respect to Gross National Product and to population, the Federal Republic of Germany has a higher than average share of world trade and one may thereby note the significance which world economic activities have for West German firms.

The development of import and export figures for the West Germany may be read from Table 4.

Table 4. Imports and exports of West Germany from 1972 to 1987[3]

Year	Actual Values					Index of Volume[1]			
	Total			per inhabitant		Total		per inhabitant	
	Imports	Exports	Export surplus	Imports	Exports	Imports	Exports	Imports	Exports
	DM (Millions)			DM		1980=100			
1972	128744	149023	+20278	2088	2416	71.5	65.6	71.4	65.5
1973	145417	178396	+32979	2346	2878	75.5	74.8	75.0	74.4
1974	179733	230578	+50846	2896	3716	72.5	83.0	71.9	82.4
1975	184313	221589	+37276	2981	3584	72.3	73.7	72.0	73.4
1976	222173	256642	+34469	3611	417	85.1	87.4	85.2	87.5
1977	235178	273614	+38436	3830	4456	87.1	90.9	87.3	91.2
1978	243707	284907	+41200	3974	4646	93.0	93.8	93.3	94.2
1979	292040	314469	+22429	4760	5125	100.0	98.3	100.4	98.7
1980	341380	350328	+8947	5545	5690	100.0	100.0	100.0	100.0
1981	369179	396898	+27720	5985	6435	95.0	106.6	94.9	106.4
1982	376464	427441	+51277	6108	6940	96.3	110.1	96.2	110.0
1983	390192	432281	+42089	6353	7038	100.1	109.8	100.4	110.0
1984	434257	488223	+53966	7099	7981	105.3	119.8	106.0	120.6
1985	463811	537164	+73353	7600	8802	109.7	126.9	110.7	128.0
1986	413744	526363	+112619	6775	8620	116.4	128.6	117.3	129.5
1987	409641	527377	+117735	6697	8621	122.7	132.3	123.5	133.2

[1] 1972 to 1975 adjusted from an original base of 1976

The data which could be ascertained by autumn indicate that in 1986 exports, in particular, will show a further significant increase. The Federal Republic of Germany is on the way to becoming the largest exporter in the world and international contracts will clearly be the motor of the country's economic growth.

[3] Taken from Statistisches Bundesamt (Ed.), Statistisches Jahrbuch 1988 für die Bundesrepublik Deutschland, Stuttgart and Mainz 1988, p.251.

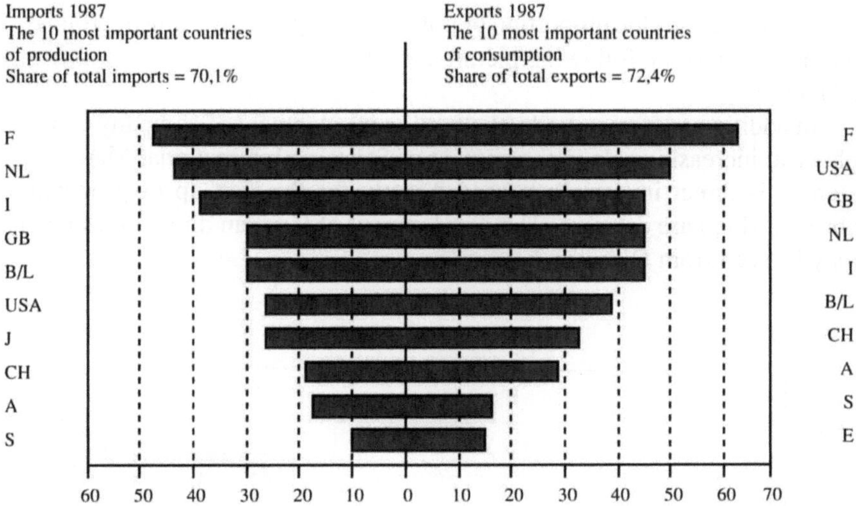

Diagram 2. The ten most important trading partners of the Federal Republic of Germany[4]

However, global information about the level of West German imports and exports sketches only a rather hazy outline of the importance of international contracts for individual branches of industry, or of contacts with specific countries. Diagram 2 therefore provides information about the most important trading partners of the Federal Republic of Germany.

Table 5. Imports and exports of the Federal Republic of Germany in 1987 arranged according to product groups[5]

	Imports		Exports	
	in DM (millions)	%	in DM (millions)	%
Food industry	51827	12,7	26397	5,0
Manufacturing industry:				
raw materials	27956	6,8	6625	1,3
semi-finished products	50994	12,4	28610	5,4
finished products, pre-products	59508	14,5	86966	16,5
finished products, end products	211000	51,5	375180	71,1

[4] Taken from Statistisches Bundesamt (Ed.), Statistisches Jahrbuch 1988 für die Bundesrepublik Deutschland, Stuttgart and Mainz 1988, p. 269.
[5] Taken from Statistisches Bundesamt (Ed.), Statistisches Jahrbuch 1988 für die Bundesrepublik Deutschland, Stuttgart and Mainz 1988, p. 252.

If one analyses the proportion of import and export according to groups of goods, one gets the following picture for 1985.
(Table 5).

In addition to foreign trade, the foreign involvement of company capital[6] plays an increasing role in the context of Strategic International Marketing. Here it is direct investments, used directly for the start-up of production abroad, which are decisive. The development of German direct investments may be seen from Diagram 3.

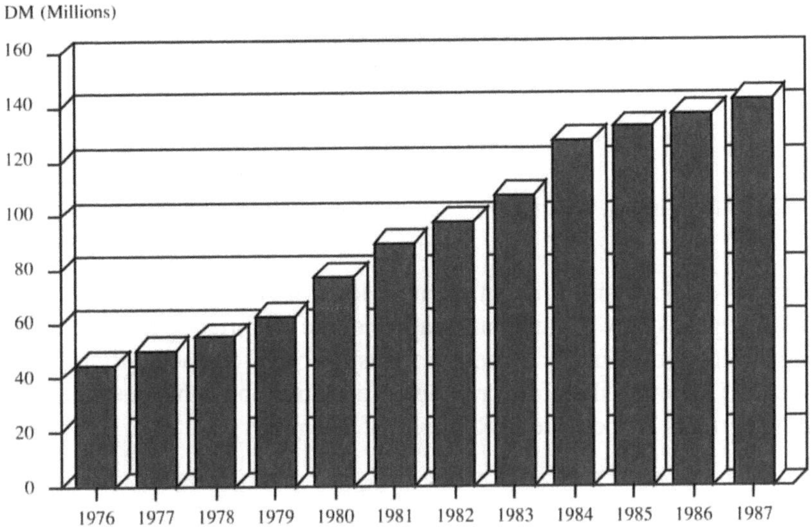

Diagram 3. The development of German direct investments abroad[7]

An overview of the status of the foreign wealth of the Federal Republic of Germany, in the form of company involvement until the end of 1983 and segmented according to groups of countries, important countries and areas of investment is given by Table 6.

From an analysis of the respective degrees of involvement, both of German direct investment abroad and of foreign direct investment in West Germany, one arrives finally at the structure of wealth indicated by Diagram 4.

---

[6] See n.a., Die Kapitalverflechtung der Unternehmen mit dem Ausland, in: Monatsberichte der Deutschen Bundesbank, vol. 33, no. 10 (Oct. 1981), pp. 39–55.

[7] Diagram based on data taken from: Institut der deutschen Wirtschaft (Ed.), Zahlen zur wirtschaftlichen Entwicklung der Bundesrepublik Deutschland, 1989, Cologne 1989, Table 115.

Table 6. The structure of direct investments[8]

The state of West German foreign holdings in company participation arranged according to groups of countries, important countries and areas of investment.
State at the end of 1987 in thousands of millions of marks.

group of countries/ country	group of countries/country: Direct German invest-ment abroad	group of countries/country: Direct foreign invest-ment in West Ger-many
EC countries including:	61,6	35,5
Belgium	6,4	1,4
France	12,8	6,6
Great Britain	8,6	9,6
Italy	7,1	1,8
Luxembourg	7,1	0,7
Netherlands	10,0	13,9
Other industrialized western countries	70,2	63,7
including:		
Japan	3,3	6,4
Canada	3,8	0,9
Austria	5,7	1,5
Sweden	0,8	2,6
Switzerland	8,1	15,8
USA	43,1	35,0
Developing countries	17,7	2,0
OPEC countries	2,4	0,7
State trade countries	0,1	0,7
totals	152,0	102,6

sector of the economy	sector of economy: Direct German invest-ment abroad	sector of economy: Direct foreign inves-ment
mining	4,8	0,2
manufacturing	69,1	59,0
including		
chemical industry	26,4	10,8
mineral oil industry	0,1	7,2
iron and steel production	1,6	1,1
engineering industry	5,8	4,4
production of office machines, data-processing machines and equipment	0,7	5,6
motor industry	10,9	5,5
electrical industry	11,9	7,1
agricultural and food industries	1,2	3,5
commercial	32,0	19,3
credit institutes	10,7	8,9
finance company	10,0	0,2
insurance company	6,0	2,1
holding companies and other property management	8,7	6,8
other services	7,2	4,2
other companies	3,5	1,9

[8] Taken from: Deutsche Bundesbank (Eds.), Monthly Reports of the German Federal Bank 1989, No. 4, p.28.

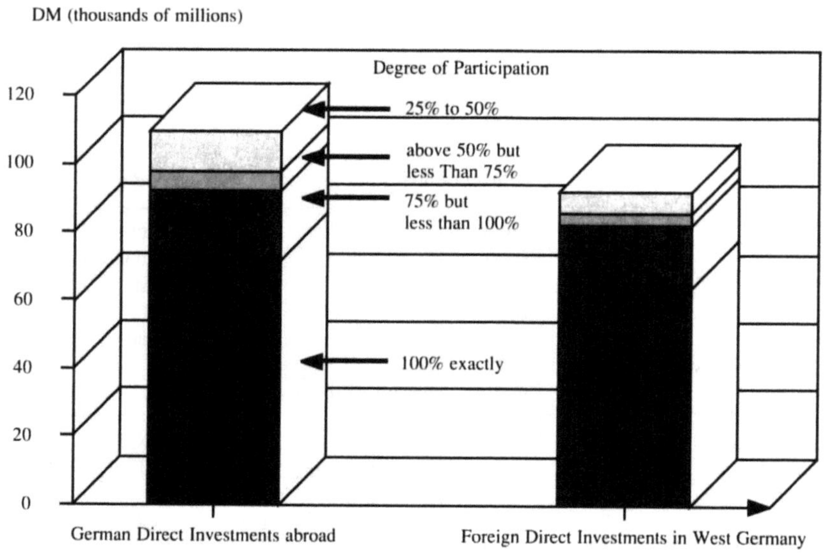

Diagram 4. Wealth structure of direct investments according to the degree of participation[9] (state at end of 1983: the diagram shows the percentage share of the investor in the nominal capital of the object of investment)

From the point of view of German companies, the decisive dynamic aspect of the development of the international division of labour is represented by the extremely intensive networking which takes place within the framework of the European Community. The trade-creating, and thus growth-promoting role of European integration becomes evident in this interweaving of imports and exports among countries with comparable economic and social structures such as France, Italy and Great Britain.

The orientation of company policy towards opportunities within the common market of the European Community represents under today's conditions one of the most self-evident prerequisites of successful company management, and has led many companies to the establishment of a special Euro-Marketing. With the addition of Spain and Portugal to the Community, this positive basic constellation has further improved for German companies.

A further essential aspect of the present international division of labour may be seen in the increasing world economic significance of the Pacific Basin. In addition to the importance of Japan, the salient features here are the world economic importance of countries such as Australia and New Zealand, and of Indonesia, Korea, Singapore, Taiwan and Malaysia and the increasing significance of the People's Republic of China.

[9] Taken from: Deutsche Bundesbank (Eds.), Monthly Reports of the German Federal Bank 1985, No. 3, p.33.

2. Political, Social and Cultural Developments

The specific dynamics of the world economy have, from the very beginning, never been determined solely or indeed exclusively by economic developments in the individual countries and regions of the world, but have at all times been subjected to the simultaneous influences of political developments, social structures and cultural factors.

When it comes to the strategic decisions of companies, political, social and cultural factors represent not just marginal conditions which attain a marginal significance as external factors, but rather these factors are the origin and the precondition for the direction and the intensity of the flow of foreign trade. The economic sciences have adopted a stance towards the influence of these factors which is short-sighted or even at times blind to the facts. The separation of economic and political factors of influence gives rise, even at the level of analysis of economic developments and therefore of entrepreneurial possibilities, to a one-sidedness which does not do justice to the complexity of economic problems. In foreign trade above all, the political, social and cultural factors must be brought along with the economic ones into the centre of the decision processes of companies or other institutions which are engaged in such trade.

One of the essential and indispensable prerequisites for the internationally oriented marketing strategies of companies is, therefore, the development of a political economy of foreign trade for companies. In the concrete world economic situation this means the consideration and evaluation of political tensions and social developments in the world. This holds true both for the major confrontations of world politics between the Western world and the centrally planned economies, and for individual local or regional areas of tension. The more important the world economic engagement of individual companies, the more strongly they will be drawn into world political confrontation, whether they want this or not.

Companies which are oriented towards foreign trade or world trade must therefore develop a particular sensitivity towards both internal and foreign political events and tendencies in the world. The possibility that companies could by themselves determine or at least influence political or social development in individual countries or regions of the world, as has been said of US combines in Central America, is practically unthinkable under the present-day structural conditions of the world economy and world politics. The growing international self-consciousness of a large number of developing countries, and also the definitive political and economic power possessed by some countries (i.e. by the OPEC countries for several years), now permit companies no more than the option of adjustment to the political situation of the respective foreign markets, if they do not wish to risk the permanent loss of a country or of a region as an actual or potential trading partner.

Social developments in the world acquire an equally decisive importance for the Strategic International Marketing of companies. Social development expresses itself most conspicuously in major political structures and in legal changes, but it also proceeds by way of far-reaching changes of consciousness and new systems of value among populations, or by revolutionary changes in the processes of information and education in individual countries. This social change takes place in different ways in the different sub-markets of the world and thus becomes an important basis for differentiation for the international marketing strategies of companies.

A further, and today increasingly important, aspect may be found in the worldwide global processes of social change. The development of a broad middle-class with typical middle-class modes of behaviour and patterns of consumption is visible today in all western industrial countries from the USA and Europe to Japan. Many of the social changes in the developing countries and in the state trade countries also follow this middle-class "way of life" of highly industrialised societies. This development transcends national borders as well as ideological barriers. The expansion of the media, particularly of television, and the simplified and intensified possibilities of travel have contributed to this development just as has the global diffusion of scientific knowledge and methods of working.

All this means that companies involved in Strategic International Marketing will have to bring a high level of attention to bear on the process of social change, and also on political developments in the world. The markets of the world and especially the markets of the future, on which companies place all hope of their continuance, are now arising in precise conjunction with social developments e.g. in the context of office automation, or of the dynamics of clothing styles or film production. But it is only the systematic grasp of social tendencies with reference to change and alteration which will open to companies the gate to an understanding of their international market opportunities.

In addition to political and social developments, cultural factors also have a profound influence on the development of the world economy. "Culture" is taken to mean the totality of the traditions and norms which delineate and determine the specificity of a defined cultural circle.[10]

The consideration of cultural factors in international marketing brings to the fore the question as to the differentiation or the unification of products and marketing strategies. The is the central problem of information, formation and

---

[10] On the concept of culture cf. especially Kluckhohn, C., Spiegel der Menschheit, Zürich 1951, and Malinowski, B., Eine wissenschaftliche Theorie der Kultur, Zürich 1949.

decision which now confronts International Marketing.[11] The problem becomes particularly evident in trade with Japan. In the face of complaints about the balance of trade surpluses of Japan as an element of disruption and of permanent disequilibrium in the world economy, Japanese companies and organisations always point out that foreign producers pay too little attention to the cultural particularities of the Japanese market. In this situation, the neglect of Japanese culture by foreign producers stretches from ignorance of the Japanese language, both spoken and written, to lack of knowledge of the particularities of the Japanese style of doing business or of centuries old traditions.[12]

Regionalism, with all the cultural differences it entails, is at present increasing in importance, in spite of rapid means of communication, comprehensive information processes and strong national states. Growing regionalism is to be understood as a reaction against the excessive nationalistic and centralistic policies of individual states from the beginning of industrialisation until the end of the Second World War.

The consequence of this for Strategic International Marketing is that one is dealing not just with questions of national differences, but simultaneously with the expression of cultural differences which often present themselves with particular sharpness and clarity precisely on the regional level; this tendency is growing both in extent and in intensity. Such regional cultural differences are now emerging in Europe too, for example in the Basque country, in Croatia, in Belgium and in Ireland. Often, these regional differences are coupled with political tensions, so that it is here above all that Strategic International Marketing must be developed in a particularly careful manner.

3. Technical Progress: Information and Communication

The dynamics of the world economy are increasingly determined by the technical progress which has been achieved in some countries of the world and is being pushed further. Technological new and further developments represent one of the essential driving forces of the dynamics of the world economy and are especially for some industrial nations with limited resources of raw

---

[11] Cf. Meffert, H., Althans, J., Internationales Marketing, Stuttgart 1982, pp. 98.

[12] Cf. Meissner, H. G., Systemvergleich zwischen deutschen und japanischen Marktstrategien, in: Gaugler, E., Meissner, H. G., Thom, N. (Eds.), Zukunftsaspekte der anwendungsorientierten Betriebswirtschaftslehre, Stuttgart 1986, pp. 211–222; Graham, J. L., Sano, Y., Smart Bargaining – Doing Business with the Japanese, Cambridge/Mass. 1984.

materials (for example West Germany or Japan) the decisive contributing factor to international competitiveness. Technological innovations and the corresponding know-how are becoming the dominant elements in the system of the international division of labour, which marks the foreign trade of many states in a decisive manner. The high proportion of investment goods in German exports, and at the same time the high proportion of investment goods in German imports, underline this influence with great emphasis.

The identification of technological gaps in the various sub-markets of the world therefore represents an increasingly important precondition for the foreign successes of companies. By comparison with this "technological exchange pattern" of modern foreign trade the "colonial exchange pattern" now plays a merely marginal role. The **colonial foreign trade pattern** is characterised by the exchange of raw materials for finished products whereby, in addition to aspects of supply, it is price relations which assume the dominant role and direct trade. With the **technological foreign trade pattern** on the other hand, it is the technological ability to solve problems which is of decisive importance, whereas considerations of price, while remaining important, are no longer the sole or one-sided determining factor. Financing strategies and the provision of services in the form of training and instruction, repairs and technical back-up determine international efficiency to an increasing degree. The international competitiveness of companies is a function of the extent of their competence in problem-solving.

The present level of technological progress is an important motor of world trade and at the same time provides essential services as a pacemaker in the bringing into being and closing of certain foreign trade deals.[13] The modern systems of information and communication play a major role here. The technological facilitation of communication has made a decisive contribution to the growth of world trade and the world economy.

Information and communication have thus become key factors not just in our technological, but also in our economic, social and cultural development. Correspondingly large is the influence which the build-up of information systems which cover various countries and world-wide communications has gained over the development of the world economy and over the formation and decision processes of the Strategic International Marketing of companies.

Concerning information, the most salient features are the possibilities offered by telecommunications and the international exchange of data. In this context one may refer to the significance of data exchange for international banking and to the importance of the electronic transmission of building

[13] Cf. Bundesministerium für Wirtschaft (Ed.), Hochtechnologien und internationale Wettbewerbsfähigkeit der deutschen Wirtschaft, Document No. 263, July 1984; also Kern, W., Zur Analyse des internationalen Transfers von Technologien, in: ZfbF, Vol. 25, pp.85–98.

designs, draughtmen's documents or the contents of tenders in the international construction industry. But in the field of communications, in spite of the highly developed information technologies, the possibility of direct and multiple personal contact continues to play the same essential role as before and this has been made possible by the expansion of world air traffic and the infrastructure of hotels, conference centres and trade fairs.

The scope of information and the speed and intensity of communication have in the course of recent years become essential factors in the dynamics of the world economy. Neither the transfer of technology nor the political, social and cultural developments which affect the world economy would be possible without this infrastructure of information systems and possibilities of communication.

C. The Structure of the International Environment of Companies

1. The Importance of Differentiated Analyses of the Environment

The peculiarity of Strategic International Marketing resides in the fact that it is not restricted to the sales and purchase markets proper, but that the environment of these markets becomes the major decision parameter.[1] It is only when environmental considerations are taken into account that strategic international marketing decisions can be made. These make special demands on the information and decision processes of companies, as environmental factors first of all present themselves in a more differentiated form than is the case on the home market, because they contain political, legal, social and cultural elements which can be taken for granted at home. Secondly, they are more varied, since the world market consists of a multitude of different national and also regional sub-markets, in each of which environmental factors bear a different stamp and have a profound importance for market opportunities and risks. The significance of environmental factors for Strategic International Marketing implies that commercial decision processes are to a large extent determined not just by national economic, world-economic and world-political factors, but also by cultural ones. The traditional dividing line between business management theory and economic theory (particularly political economy), thereby loses its significance. There arises rather a typical continuum of micro- and macroeconomic determining factors.

The structure of the complex international environment may be demonstrated as follows in Table 7.

To a considerable extent traditional foreign trade theory concentrated its attention merely on the particularities of the natural environment in the form of climatic and geographical conditions. By contrast, the partner-oriented theory of the foreign activities of companies brings in the totality of environ-

---

[1] Cf. Dülfer, E., Zum Problem der Umweltberücksichtigung im "Internationalen Management", in: Pausenberger, E. (Ed.), Internationales Management, Stuttgart 1981, pp.1–44.

Table 7. The structure of the international environment

Environmental Factor / Countries or Country Groups	the natural enviro-ment	economic develop-ments	technolo-gical standard	legal and political system	the cultural framework
1. Memberstates of the EC – France – Great Britain – Italy – …					
2. EFTA-Countries – Austria – Norway – …					
3. Other industrial countries – USA – Japan – Canada – …					
4. Threshold Countries – Turkey – South Korea – Brazil					
5. OPEC-Countries – Saudi Arabien – Mexico – …					
6. Other Developing Countries – Albania – Peru – Chad – …					
7. State Trade Countries – Poland – China – Cuba					

mental factors which are relevant to the preparation, closing and further development of foreign trade deals.

A structural analysis of the international environment of companies must of necessity take into account the legal, political and cultural frameworks and the socio-economic state of development of individual countries, and also investigate their trade and currency policies. This entails expanded information requirements and specific evaluation processes.

In the discussion of environmental factors, it is important to note that the processes of integration within the European Community are of special importance for German and for other European companies. The member states of the EC took up just 48% of all German exports in 1984 and similarly the Federal Republic of Germany drew 48% of its imports from EC countries.[2] With a share of 12.6% of German exports and of 10.6% of imports, France is the largest trading partner of the Federal Republic, just as the Federal Republic is the largest trading partner of France. As a result of the trade-promoting effects of the EC, a situation which is analogous to that of home market has arisen throughout the Community. The environment of the EC thus approaches the conditions which prevail within the home market of the Federal Republic of Germany. Nevertheless, in spite of this integrative development the social and cultural differences remain in the individual sub-markets.[3] Moreover, the national, legal and currency systems still persist. But yet the differences are less intense than is the case between member states and non-member states.

2. Sociocultural Development and Economic Growth

Socio-economic developments in the major zones of the world market represent the decisive environmental condition for the development of foreign trade and thus for the prognosis of future sales potential. Economic growth, the development of trade cycles, taxation policy, the distribution policy pursued and above all currency policy in the important foreign markets are all becoming factors which substantially influence the export opportunities of companies, as well as any possibilities they might have of other foreign

[2] Cf. Deutsche Bundesbank (Ed.), Statistische Beihefte zu den Monatsberichten der Deutschen Bundesbank, Series 3, Zahlungsbilanzstatistik. No. 6, (June 1985), p.10.

[3] See for example the discussion of the sociocultural peculiarities of the Netherlands by Ernest Zahn in: Zahn, E., Das unbekannte Holland, Berlin 1984.

activities. The connection between economic growth and sociocultural change is of particularly great significance for the development of foreign business.

Technological development, with the attendant opportunities to increase productivity, is leading in all industrial countries as well as in a large number of threshold and developing countries to processes of clear economic growth in real terms. Even a world-wide interruption of the trade cycle, such as was registered in 1982, was unable to halt further economic growth.

A special dynamic of growth is to be noted among the Southeast Asian nations, which exhibit growth rates between 8% and over 10%.[4] The substantial economic growth of Southeast Asia has two different consequences both for German and for Japanese foreign trade: on the one hand considerable sales markets are growing in these countries for German and Japanese manufacturers, and on the other it is precisely the threshold countries of this region which are increasingly emerging as competitors on third markets, such as the USA or Latin America. A process of growth which differs markedly across regions is thereby linked to a noticeable structural change in the world economy. For the foreign activities of companies, it is therefore important not just to spot the immediately obvious chances of economic growth, but also to become aware of precisely such processes of structural change. To that extent one-dimensional input-output relations as predictions of the future division of labour in the world economy cannot adequately cope with this dynamic aspect of world economic growth. They must be replaced by models of explanation and decision which give the most comprehensive consideration possible to the various types of network of cause and effect and interdependence.

The systematic interrelationship of economic growth, structural change in the world economy and sociocultural changes makes it particularly difficult to make unequivocal quantitative predictions about the future flow of world trade, especially as these are further influenced by additional factors, such as the relations of foreign currency exchange rates, or internal or foreign political events. Long-term forecasting in foreign business should therefore concern itself above all else with the recognition of relevant patterns in the world economy: the structures of development must be made transparent and the consequences analysed for the development of the foreign business of individual companies. What is called for here is not any pseudo-exact quantification of single developments, but the discovery of the systematic interconnections between the dominant factors and the tendencies which influence them; this must be done with plausibility and a high degree of reliability. They must then be interpreted with reference to their relevance for future developments, without any ideological reservations or wishful thinking.

[4] Cf. on this point the various contributions in: Laumer, H. (Ed.), Wachstumsmarkt Südostasien, Munich, Cologne, London 1984.

The techniques to interpret such complex developments in the world economy have been devised by futurology. Futurology concerns itself with the creation of scenarios of probable future development.[5] These scenarios are based on various assumptions, such as certain courses of growth. On this basis plausible developments can then be partially quantified, which is done primarily by means of an analysis of the probabilities of the future occurrence of certain developments and events. In this context, one must of course always bear in mind that the quantification of a future development in the world economy has come into being by way of various qualitative assumptions, concerning, for example, a certain structural change.

Economic growth always triggers processes of social change too, particularly those which arise in connection with distribution struggles. The economic growth of Japan did not, for example, lead to the ruling social class of the Samurai families becoming even richer and more powerful on its own, but to Japan's developing a noticeable middle class and corresponding patterns of middle class behaviour. The identity of the Japanese nation is created particularly by the normative force of the middle class consciousness.[6]

The processes of economic growth are also linked to changes of consciousness and of the value system. This expresses itself in, among other things, a changed life-style, which in turn brings about a change or an adjustment in consumer habits and in consumer expenditure. International Marketing must therefore of necessity analyse these processes of world economic growth and of the structural change connected with it. Companies cannot therefore content themselves with quantitative analyses of is and ought conditions, but must bring the sociocultural background of these developments into their analysis.

The growth of the world economy and sociocultural change today take place in three different segments of the world market, each of which exhibits a different growth dynamic as well as a different dynamic of sociocultural change. These three segments are:

- the traditional industrial countries (with the special role of the EC countries),
- the developing countries (including the significance which the threshold countries and the OPEC states possess within this group of countries),
- the state trade countries, which have organised themselves economically in Comecon, over which the Soviet Union claims hegemony.

---

[5] Cf. on the scenario method e.g. Kahn, H., World Economic Development, New York 1979, pp. 503 ff.

[6] Cf. Ballon, R. J.(Ed.), Japan's Market and Foreign Business, Tokyo 1971, especially pp. 107 ff. the chapter "The Japanese Consumer".

Economic growth in the **western industrial countries** (including Japan) has contributed in a far-reaching manner to the development of a changing system of values in these countries. The elites find themselves in an increasing crisis of legitimisation, which pressurises them into having to justify their behaviour in specific situations. The media in these countries have played a part in placing not only all political, but also the economic positions of power, under this permanent legitimisation pressure. The publicity work of companies has therefore attained in these countries a position which has become particularly important from the strategic point of view. In many cases marketing rides upon the tracks which have been laid down by the publicity work of companies and associations.

In the industrial countries the working careers of men and women are increasingly coming to represent only a limited episode in the lives of many people. The course of life is dominated in time by education at one end and retirement at the other. The time of professional activity is shrinking to a period of transience. The value system of many citizens of the highly industrialised countries is undergoing a corresponding change, along with their lifestyle and consumer habits. Freedom is being associated with free time and the quality of life is becoming the ruling paradigm of the "Affluent Society".

But associated with this development, one also finds a critique of culture which drives, in the face of material superfluity, towards inwardness and self-limitation right up to the point of asceticism. In this context sects of a Far Eastern stamp have found a large following among younger people who seek other goals than the orientation of their lives towards the realisation of material security and the ideals of wealth and the consumer patterns of a bourgeois society.

The economic growth which has been attained and which is still continuing in the industrial countries and the quality of life which is associated with it have led to far-reaching processes of sociocultural change. What is noticeable here is not just that the direction of change leads in the first instance to a widespread smoothing-out of values and patterns of behaviour in the industrial countries and thus to the formation of supranational market segments, but that simultaneously a consciousness for certain specific cultural qualities is growing as a reaction against such a smoothing-out. International marketing must therefore develop a specific sensitivity for the processes of economic growth and of change, in order to be able to make both realistic assumptions about future developments in the industrial countries and the decisions which these assumptions require.

In the **developing countries** one is witnessing the rise of a new technocratic elite which is characterised by self-consciousness and ambition. Here too a thoroughgoing process of sociocultural change is under way, in the dissolution of the traditional elites with the scales of values which they have had handed down, and which are out-of-date with respect to the problem complexes they now have to face. In a number of developing countries this has led to a massive cultural conflict, which is then connected with internal political confrontations and revolutionary upheavals. A model of this development is presented by the situation in Iran. Here, the technocratic style of sovereign authority espoused by the Shah was brought down by the tradition-conscious Mullahs. Other developing countries too find themselves caught in a typical internal confrontation, as they try to find their own identity between tradition and progress.

In many developing countries, one finds a clear disparity between the urban and the rural populations. The urban population, especially in the great metropoles of the Third World, follows to a remarkably great extent the scales of values and consumption patterns which have been set up by the western industrial nations. The rural population, on the other hand, has up to now remained largely excluded from further technological and economic development, and its members live out their lives within a social framework which has persisted for many centuries. There thus arises between the urban and the rural populations a disparity of development and of scales of values, which has led in many developing countries to an economic and social dualism. Decisions in international marketing must not fail to take this dualism into account.

The **threshold countries** occupy a quite conspicuous special position in the economic and social development of the world. By threshold countries, such as Korea and Singapore, Israel and Mexico, Brazil and Yugoslavia, are meant those countries which stand on the threshold of industrialisation and which already enjoy an income per head of the population which approaches the standard achieved by the industrial countries in preceding periods. The threshold countries are making strenuous efforts to break into the world economic division of labour and thus to create the preconditions required for their further economic growth. In order to secure their international competitiveness and further integration into the world-wide system of labour division and trade relationships, it is these countries above all others which are prepared to accept foreign capital and, in particular, foreign know-how in the areas both of technology and of management. Threshold countries thus represent important target areas for foreign investments. Thus the threshold countries of Southeast Asia have become the preferred target of Japanese foreign investment. Here German and European companies must answer the question as to whether they have up to now neglected developments in these countries, so that they are in the long run being squeezed out of these markets.[7]

---

[7] Cf. Kebschull, D., Ausländische Direktinvestitionen in Südostasien – ein internationaler Vergleich des Engagements in: Laumer, H. (Ed.), Wachstumsmarkt Südostasien, Munich, Cologne, London 1984, pp. 435–463.

The social dynamic of the threshold countries is characterised by a particular state of unrest. As the Western quality of life is reached, the populations of these countries strive also for the realisation of the political culture of the western industrial nations in their own countries. Many threshold countries strive after a form of representative democracy. Political developments in Spain after the death of the previous Head of State Franco make clear this tendency to bring into being a democratic form of government to match a certain level of achievement of economic growth and relative prosperity. The internationalisation of the media and the opportunities of world-wide communication help to speed up this process of the establishment of a democratic basic order.

The **state trade countries** occupy a further special position in the world economy. The centrally planned economic organisation of these countries and the bureaucratisation of foreign trade which this entails make it very difficult for these countries to integrate themselves fully into the processes of the world economic division of labour. They therefore concentrate on foreign trade between the member states of COMECON and utilise the advantages of the international division of labour for only restricted sections of their output spectrum. In the area of sales marketing it is primarily only through exports, usually with a share of compensations in order to pay for imports, that the state trade countries participate in the international division of labour; and it is also only from exports (at dumping prices when necessary) that results are expected for employment and foreign currency policies. In the area of purchase marketing the COMECON countries allow themselves to be guided by investment gaps in their industrial companies, by the need to maintain their production and to achieve an increase in productivity. The low level of integration into the world economy can therefore lead only slowly to sociocultural consequences in these countries. It is possible that the close connection between economic and sociocultural change is the reason why the governments of the state trade countries are dilatory in promoting a more intensive integration into the world economy.

The **triad** arose as a consequence of these developments in the world.[8] This world economic triad has developed between the USA, Japan and the EC, and within the EC the central role is played by the Federal Republic of Germany. The greater part of world trade takes place within this triad. An intensive networking of companies has grown up within the triad, as has, in the meantime, a common consciousness among the triad's citizens. In the context of the dynamics of the world economy, the differences between Americans, Japanese and Europeans are becoming smaller. This process of a world-wide integration of various cultures is triggered in particular by the orientation of

[8] Cf. Ohmae, K., Die Macht der Triade, Wiesbaden 1985.

the citizens within the triad towards technical progress. Since technical progress is international, the ways of behaviour and value systems of people are also structuring themselves internationally to an increasing degree.

3. Legal, Political and Cultural Environmental Conditions

The international environment, which acts upon the informational, organisational and decision processes of companies, is characteristically composed not just of economic and trade-political factors, but is determined by precisely that total complex of legal, political and cultural factors which influences the events of the world economy. The opportunities as well as the risks for companies involved in foreign trade thus arise in an environment which is very

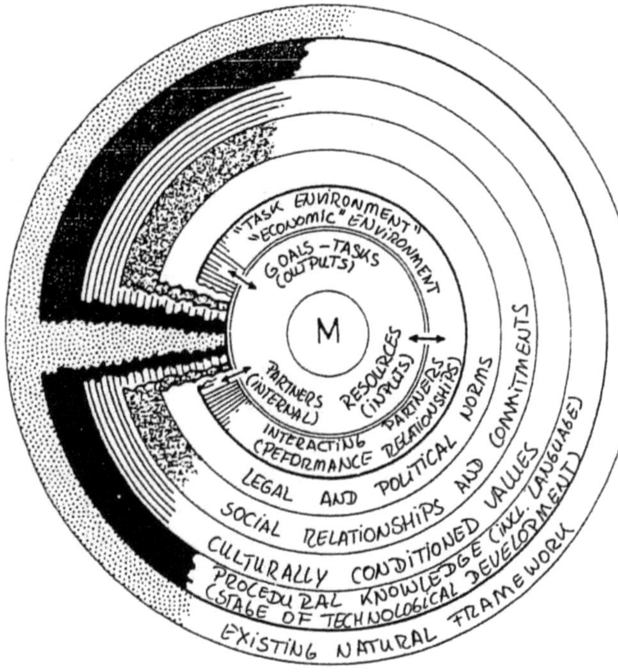

Diagram 5. Layer model of environmental differentiation[9]

[9] Taken from: Dülfer, E, Zum Problem der Umweltberücksichtigung im "Internationalen Management", in: Pausenberger, E. (Ed.), Internationales Management, Stuttgart 1981, p.31.

much more complex and more demanding than is encountered on the home market. The extent of this external influence on company decisions is without any historical parallel. The total complex of environmental factors introduces a new, additional dimension into the decision processes of companies, and it is a dimension which has been seen – if at all – merely as a marginal phenomenon by traditional business management theory. New fields of operation thus open themselves up for the strategic options of companies. This tendency becomes particularly clear in the orientation of companies towards Strategic International Marketing.

The consideration of the environment has become a core problem for International Management. The companies concerned therefore have to consider the special legal, political and cultural environmental conditions when making decisions in International Management and International Marketing. Internationally active companies are embedded in every case in a concrete environment, which Dülfer has presented in the form of a layer model.

Legal framework conditions exhibit a very different structure in many countries. Thus for example, by comparison with German law, extended producer liability in the USA represents a considerable economic risk. Foreign activities should therefore be supervised by specialist lawyers. This is particularly true when founding or extending affiliates abroad or when sealing licensing or patent agreements.[10]

The situation is particularly difficult for companies when it comes to analysing political environmental conditions and future political developments in the individual regions and sub-markets of the world. Political environmental conditions refer to internal as well as to foreign political developments. Internal political tensions often force foreign firms to adopt appropriate stances. The companies thus find themselves very quickly confronting the political opposition in a country. When a change of government or processes of a revolutionary nature occur, then the companies find themselves cast once more in an oppositional role which they have not sought and which, in the interests of their long-term business relationships with the country concerned, they do not want. On the other hand, premature contacts with oppositional groups can easily bring the companies into an unenviable position with respect to the powers that be. One then hears the accusation of foreign companies meddling in the internal affairs of the country, and there are negative consequences for the commercial freedom of action and for the image of the company concerned. The behaviour of foreign companies in

[10] Cf. Arbeitskreis Karenberg/Meissner der Schmalenbach-Gesellschaft: "Auslandsaktivitäten deutscher Unternehmen", Cologne (Bundesstelle für Außenhandelsinformationen) 1983, p. 71.

situations of internal political tension represents a particularly difficult area for companies in the process of their adjustment to the world economic scene. Examples may be found in the present world economic situation from Central America to South Africa to the Middle East.

From the very beginning, foreign political tensions in the world have presented a profound hindrance to trade, particularly when these are connected with the actual use of force or with boycott measures. Foreign political tension equally forces companies to adopt stances which they do not seek or care for with their long-term orientation in mind. In cases of the escalation of foreign political tensions to military conflict, the companies are confronted by a specific political risk. It is true that this risk can be partially covered by insurance. However, there remains the structural political risk, which touches upon the existence of companies in a politically unsettled country. The latent political risk which precedes military confrontations and which may under certain circumstances last for a very long time cannot be covered by the present-day insurance system. This political risk is to be counted among the significant strategic foreign trade risks faced by companies. Companies must therefore concern themselves with making such strategic decisions as.minimise this foreign political risk or balance it out within an international framework.

Rather than the framework conditions provided by the natural environment, which played an important role in traditional foreign trade theory,[11] it is today those of the cultural environment which are coming to occupy the primary attentions of companies which are oriented towards foreign trade. The significance of cultural factors for the dynamics of the world economy has already been discussed. Here it is necessary to stress once more the importance of the cultural conditions which provide the framework for the information, structuring and decision procedures of companies.

The strategic concept of companies oriented towards foreign trade must at all costs be so structured as to take social and cultural differentiation in the individual markets and sub-markets of the world into consideration. Even the most modern technology is employed in concrete sociocultural situations. With consumer goods or those investment goods which are closely related to consumption, such as heavy goods vehicles or office machinery, these cultural shades of difference play a particularly important role. It is true that in today's world there is a growing cultural common ground which has come into being as a result of the internationalisation of the media and improved and expanded communications. Nevertheless, the central task of International Marketing remains that of doing justice to cultural particularities and differences.

---

[11] Cf. Hellauer, J., Welthandelslehre, Wiesbaden 1950, p. 35.

Under the present-day exchange conditions of the world market companies must devote very much more attention to the development and realisation of each of their national strategies than was the case in earlier periods of economic development. The more international competition is displaced onto technical efficiency, production quality and intregrated problem-solving, and price competition thereby relativised, the more the cultural sensitisation of companies becomes the decisive factor of competition policy in International Marketing.

The importance of the cultural environmental conditions makes it imperative that companies consider these variables in a systematic manner. This is made possible by a matrix (Table 8) which relates the cultural variables to the individual international marketing functions.

Table 8. The consideration of cultural environmental conditions in International Marketing[12]

International Marketing Functions / Cultural Variables	Product Development	Pricing Policy	Sales Promotion and Advertising	Trading Channels	Market Research
1. Manifest Culture 2. Educational System 3. Language 4. Aesthetic Norms 5. Political Attitudes and Values 6. Social Organisations					

4. Trade and Currency Policy (Foreign Trade Regime)

The foreign trade regime encompasses the entire system of existing legal rules and regulations which affect the foreign trade decisions of companies. This involves the legal regulations in the country of origin and the rules in the partner country, for example, the regulations for exports from West Germany and those affecting imports into the USA. This bilateral foreign trade regime is complemented in the present-day world economy and in part also superse-

[12] Cf. on this point Terpstra, V., International Marketing, 3rd. Edn., Chicago 1983, p. 112.

ded by supranational regulations and international foreign trade prescriptions (Table 9).

Table 9. Matrix of the foreign trade regime

Areas of activity / Foreign Trade Regulations	Exports and Imports	Services	Licences and Patents	Foreign Investments		Other Transfers of Capital	Foreign Taxation Law
				Affiliates	Joint Ventures		
1. National Regulations in the Country of Origin							
2. National Regulations in the Partner Country							
3. Bilateral Regulations							
4. Supranational Regulations							
5. International Regulations							

As far as the trade of West Germany and thus the international marketing decisions of its companies are concerned, the Foreign Trade Law of 1961 set out to regulate all activities relating to the foreign trade of that country.

In Article 1 of the Foreign Trade Law the principle is established of the freedom of foreign trade activity:

> "The trade in goods, services, capital and payments and all other commercial activities with foreign economic regions, as well as trade in foreign holdings and gold between those resident in the state (foreign trade activity) is in principle free. It is subject to the restrictions which this law contains or which may be imposed by legal decree based on this law."

The restrictions, for example in trade with COMECON countries or in armaments, are guided by the foreign trade regulations of 1961 and subsequent alterations and adjustments.

Bilateral regulations represent two-sided agreements which are aimed at promoting trade between two countries and avoiding imbalances in trade and in the balance of payments. Such bilateral trade and payment agreements are made nowadays especially with the state trade countries, whereas foreign trade activity in the western world is regulated by multilateral trade and payment agreements.

In the western world, international regulations, together with the integration process within the EC, have gained in significance for trade politics. In the exchange of goods this has been achieved by the stipulations of the GATT, and in the capital and payment sector by the IMF. The General Agreement on Tariffs and Trade (GATT) is a multinational intergovernmental treaty agreed within the framework of the United Nations and with the aim of dismantling obstructions to international trade. Through various customs commissions of the GATT, the member states have striven with success to dismantle the customs-related restrictions on foreign trade activity. In its current phase of development, the GATT is also working on the task of reducing the non-tariff trade barriers. The growth which has been achieved in the last 20 years in the world economy is due not least to the successful multilateral policies of the GATT.

The task of the International Monetary Fund (IMF) consists in the promotion of international co-operation in currency policy, the easing of the expansion of world trade and the securing of orderly monetary relationships between the member-states. In order to fulfil this task the IMF has created special drawing rights which are meant to help maintain international liquidity. In the present state of the world economy the most urgent task facing the IMF is the solution of the international debt crisis.[13]

Moreover, in order to regulate various sensitive world markets, further international agreements were entered into, for example, for coffee, tea, wheat, sugar, textiles and tin. These agreements are meant to ensure a continuous supply of these raw materials to the world, but above all to protect the producers from overproduction and a consequent world-wide drop in prices. However, the interests of individual producer countries have up to now prevented these agreements from being able in the longterm to stabilise the proceeds to exporters of these commodities, a task which also failed for oil within the confines of OPEC policy.

This influence of economic, trade and currency policy on export and import decisions may be systematised as presented in Diagram 6.

---

[13] Cf. Meissner, H. G., Singer, H., Jahn, W., Banning, Th. E., Die internationale Verschuldung als Problem der Unternehmensführung, Vol. 237 of the series of publications of the Wissenschaftliche Arbeitsgemeinschaft für Technik und Wirtschaft des Landes Nordrhein-Westfalen, Dortmund 1985.

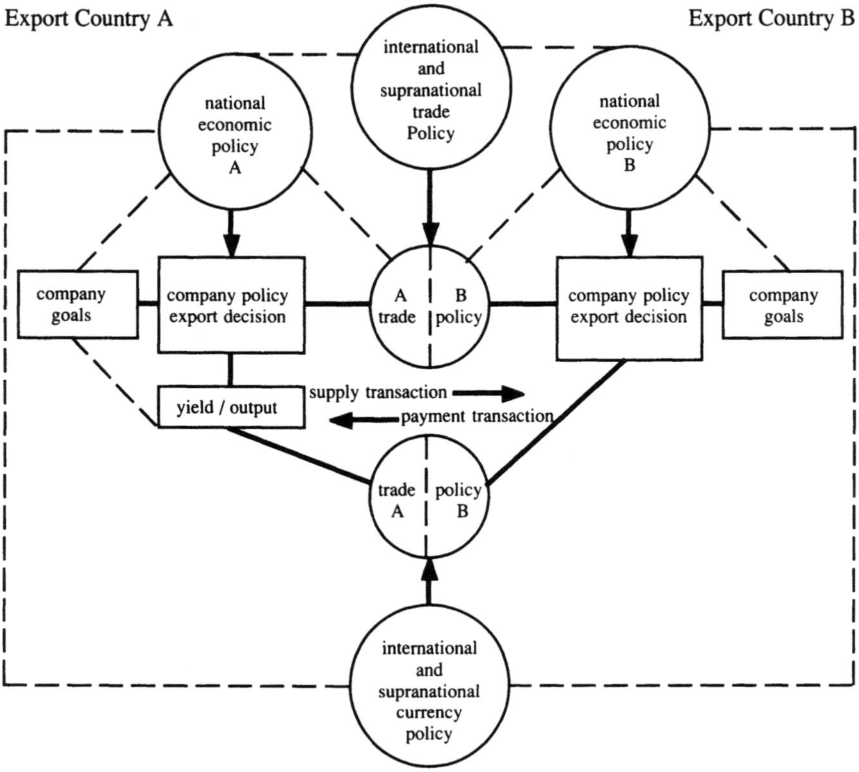

Diagram 6. The influence of economic, commercial and currency policies on the export decisions of companies[14]

For companies oriented towards foreign trade, a knowledge of the individual regulations and restrictions of the foreign trade regime is an important prerequisite for an economically successful participation in the international division of labour. For these companies and not least for the participating foreign trade banks, it is important to find out any changes in the foreign trade regime which have been introduced by individual states or by international organisations, in order to incorporate these into current decision-making. In addition to this it is becoming more and more important for multinational companies and international combines and for those companies which display a higher than average export quota to be informed about such changes well in advance, in order to be able to undertake some possible change in company policy in good time and in the long term.

[14] Taken from Meissner, H.G., Exportpolitik vom Standpunkt der Unternehmensführung, Herne and Berlin 1974, p. 35.

5. Integration Policy

The realisation of the European Community represents a substantial basis for the networking into foreign trade of German companies and of companies in the other partner states. Even companies in the two new member states of the EC, Spain and Portugal, find themselves confronted by the necessity, but also by the special opportunity, of orienting their company strategy towards the market of the European Community.

With the realisation of the European Community, important parts of the autonomy of the member states in trade policy were transferred to the European Commission in Brussels. The Common Market is an economic union within which customs duties are no longer levied and which imposes a common foreign excise tariff. This customs union is complemented by the stipulations of the European Community Treaty concerning the free mobility of persons, the freedom to establish businesses and the freedom of transfer of capital. Furthermore, the EC has developed a common trade policy and a common currency policy. Regulations concerning trade policy with the USA and Japan are becoming an increasingly important component of the common trade policy. The common trade policy also serves to harmonise the bilateral arrangements of the individual member countries with state trade countries or individual developing countries.

Within the context of the common monetary policy, the European Monetary System (EMS) was developed from 1979 onwards. Linked to the EMS there is an intervention mechanism (in which Great Britain does not participate) which is meant to reduce currency fluctuations within the Community. The ECU has been introduced as the European unit of currency.

The figures relating to the world economic networking of German industry have made clear how intensive the international division of labour within the EC has already become, and how great is that special dynamic which has been introduced via the EC into the participating national economies and thereby into companies. The integration will be pushed even further in the future, particularly by the efforts towards harmonisation in the EC. What is at issue here is the approximation of the legal systems, the unification of book-keeping and accounting regulations and the harmonisation of policies relating to taxation, transport, social matters and energy. An important part in European integration is also played by the growing co-operation in the fields of science and research.

The Common Agricultural Policy is in a special position as regards foreign trade. The agricultural policy aims at ensuring supplies to the Community and at stabilising incomes in agriculture. The increasing levels of self-sufficiency and of partial over-production, for example, in milk production, has led to a decline in the significance of the EC as an importer of agricultural products and indeed to its own emergence as a supplier on third markets. The current debt problems of individual developing countries and their trade imbalances are also an indirect result of the "success" of the Common Agricultural Policy.

D. The Foreign Activities of Companies

1. Types of Foreign Involvement and their Strategic Significance

Companies are developing their foreign activities in greater measure than before, against a background of the world economic dynamic as described above and the international division of labour which derives from it. The increase in foreign activities may be seen especially in the increase in export quotas which single companies and whole branches of manufacturing and service industries have achieved.

That portion of the turnover of goods produced in the country of origin which is sold abroad is referred to as the export quota. For some years in succession now the turnover in export sales of German industry has exhibited a rising trend. The exports quotas of West German firms have climbed along with export turnover. This means that individual firms and whole branches of business, especially in mechanical engineering and plant construction, in vehicle production and in the chemical industry are increasingly dependent on the development of foreign markets and on the opening-up of new markets abroad.

The export quota of German industry has developed as follows in recent years (Table 10).

Table 10. The export development of German industry[1]

	1984	1985	1986	1987
Export quota	28.8%	29.6%	29.7%	29.7%

[1] Data taken from: Statistisches Bundesamt (Ed.), Statistisches Jahrbuch 1988 für die Bundesrepublik Deutschland, Stuttgart and Mainz 1988, p. 176.

Behind these overall relationships, there lie three different developments:

- a further expansion of the export business of the large West German firms which are already internationally active (for example in the areas of the chemical industry, the vehicle industry and the iron and steel industry),
- an increase in the export quotas of a large number of medium-sized companies which belong to the traditionally export-oriented branches of industry (for example, in mechanical engineering, in the clothing industry and also in the foodstuffs sector) owing to an increasingly international consciousness among medium-sized companies[2],
- a consistent build-up and expansion of export business in those branches in which the percentage of exports was insignificant until a few years ago (for example, in high-tech areas such as EDP and air transport or in the furniture industry).

The individual branches of German business exhibit the following export quotas for 1984 (Table 11).

Table 11. Export quotas according to branch in 1987[3]

– Mining	10,4%
– Raw materials and manufactured goods industries	29,0%
Iron and steel industry	35,9%
Nonferrous metal production and semi-finished nonferrous tools	31,2%
Chemical industry	42,2%
– Investment goods industry	39,4%
Mechanical engineering	44,2%
Roadvehicle production	47,2%
Shipbuilding	60,7%
Aerospace construction	53,3%
Electrotechnology	31,2%
Precision engineering, optical products, clocks	37,1%
Office machinery, EDP equipment	53,7%
– Consumer goods industry	19,7%
– Food and drink industry	8,8%

[2] Cf. Arbeitskreis Karenberg/Meissner der Schmalenbach-Gesellschaft, Auslandsaktivitäten deutscher Unternehmen, eine Chance der Zukunftssicherung, Cologne, (Bundesstelle für Außenhandelsinformation) 1983.

[3] Data taken from: Statistisches Bundesamt (Ed.), Statistisches Jahrbuch 1988 für die Bundesrepublik Deutschland, Stuttgart and Mainz 1988, p. 176.

In the course of recent years, the foreign trade dynamic has transmitted itself increasingly to medium-sized companies as well. Medium-sized companies are in the first instance indirectly involved in foreign trade, especially as suppliers to international concerns, for example, in the motor vehicle industry. But they are also increasingly involved directly in export trade and are even in the meantime extending their activities in individual cases to undertake foreign investment.[4] The development of export quotas and of exports of branches of industry which are primarily structured around medium-sized companies may be read from Table 12.

Table 12. Exports of branches of industry of mainly medium-sized structure[5]

	Medium-sized companies %[1]	Export quota[2] 1984	Exports in DM (thousands of millions) 1970	1980	1983	1984	1985[3]
Mechanical engineering	93	47	24,2	57,3	64,2	68,7	77,0
Electrotechnology	88	33	12,1	34,4	41,8	48,5	53,0
Precision mechanics[4]	97	38	2,7	6,9	7,8	8,7	10,0
Fine ceramics	86	35	0,9	1,5	1,6	1,7	1,8
Musical instruments[5]	99	33	1,0	4,2	4,0	4,3	4,5
Treatment of plastics	97	23	1,9	6,2	8,0	9,3	10,7
Leather production	99	27	0,3	0,5	0,7	0,9	1,0

[1] Number of companies of less than 500 employees as a percentage of all companies in 1984
[2] Foreign sales as a proportion of total sales in %
[3] Estimated
[4] Including optical products and watches
[5] Including toys and jewelry

If the growth and extent of the export quotas can by themselves make clear the high significance of exports for the economic development of West Germany and of individual branches of industry, then this significance takes on an existential dimension when one considers individual companies.

Table 13 lists in order of importance the 15 largest West German exporters. Of these six exhibit export sales between 22 and 23 thousand million marks, and all 15 together exported goods to a value of 270 thousand million marks in 1984. If one ignores Veba , then the proportion of exports varies between 50% and 80% with eight companies selling more then 2/3 of their production abroad.

---

[4] Cf. on this point the articles in No. 6, 1985 of the BFuP with contributions by Dülfer, Steinmann, Kumar, Hielscher and Schildbach, and with statements of position by Albach, Barth, Meissner, Petzke and Schneider.

[5] Taken from: Dresdner Bank (Ed.), Wirtschaftsberichte, Vol. 37, No. 3 (Sept. 1985), p. 4.

Table 13. The 15 largest exporters[6]

	Exports in 1984 in thousands of millions DM	Exports as a proportion of company turnover in %
Bayer	33,8	78,6
Hoechst	31,2	75,3
Volkswagen	31,0	67,9
Daimler	28,8	66,3
BASF	26,4	60,7
Siemens	23,4	51,0
Thyssen	16,5	51,0
BMW	12,0	73,0
Mannesmann	10,7	68,0
Preussag	10,5	76,2
Bosch	9,7	53,0
Thyssen Handelsunion	9,5	55,9
VEBA	9,4	18,9
Alfred Töpfer	8,9	75,0
Friedr. Krupp	8,4	46,0

The foreign activities of companies are not, however, restricted to the export of goods produced in the home country, but spread themselves across various spheres, from exports to the 100% establishment of affiliates abroad. Thereby the strategic orientation of the companies shifts in several respects from the country of origin to the host country. Whereas with export business the essential efforts of management are made in the country of origin, in the case of the affiliates this takes place in the host country. Similarly any infusion of capital linked to foreign activities leads in the case of exports almost totally to a binding of financial resources in the home country, but with the affiliates on the other hand to a binding in the host country. Joint ventures, in which the investing company has undertaken only participation , and then perhaps only a minority participation, in a foreign country lie in the middle range of this spectrum which streches between the binding of capital and management involvement in the country of origin and in the host country (Diagram 7).

The systematisation of foreign activities may be undertaken with reference to three important criteria:[7]

- the degree of commitment of resources
- the degree of autonomy of the organisational unit abroad
- the nature and form of the transfer of resources.

[6] Cf. the presentation of the Deutscher Instituts-Verlag, taken from the Handelsblatt of 14.01.1986.

[7] Cf. Arbeitskreis Karenberg/Meissner der Schmalenbach-Geselschaft, Auslandsaktivitäten deutscher Unternehmen, Chancen der Zukunftssicherung, Cologne, (Bundesstelle für Außenhandelsinformation) 1983, p. 3.

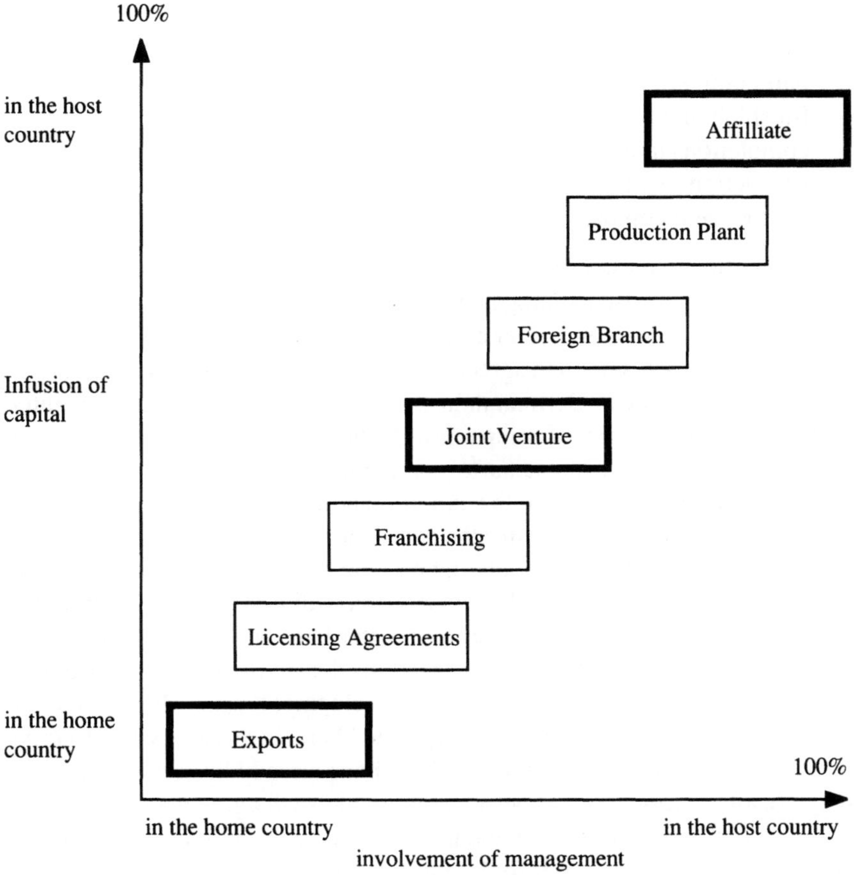

Diagram 7. Degrees of internationalisation related to the involvement of capital and of management in the country of origin and in the host country

There result from this 10 different types of foreign activity which may not, however, be strictly separated from each other. The individual types of foreign activity frequently give rise to overlappings and mixed types. If one follows in principle the proposed model of the increasing displacement of management involvement to the foreign country, then the following forms may be distinguished:[8]

- free representative
- resident
- distribution or purchasing company

[8] Cf. Arbeitskreis Karenberg/Meissner, op. cit., pp. 4–12.

- service point
- assembly works
- part completion
- finishing and planning
- completions under contract (passive involvement in finishing of goods)
- production plant
- independent company.

In addition to these institutionalised forms of foreign activity other forms of cooperation are also gaining in importance, especially through the completion of licensing deals and other agreements relating to the transfer of know-how. On the import side such agreements have the function of making foreign know-how available to German industry, which in turn safeguards the international competitiveness of companies. On the export side it serves to limit the risk which investment presents to companies, a risk which grows as the volume of trade increases and the export markets become more critical. This must be seen as necessary against the background of the liquidity problems of certain countries and a corresponding passing of laws calculated to check or stop the transfer of profits. However a precondition here is that royalties themselves do not become subject to transfer bans as is already the case in some countries. Since however governments detach their countries from the process of international technological development when they forbid the payment of royalties, they are basically quite liberal in this area when it comes to upholding licensing agreements which have already been made, but then they are all the more critical before authorising such agreements.

The combination of export and import deals with foreign investment has acquired a central importance for Strategic International Marketing. The long-term decision of companies centres largely on the question as to whether a foreign market should be opened up or extended by export dealings or by undertaking foreign investment. These alternatives must be studied with reference to both risks and opportunities and while keeping company resources and competitive conditions constantly in mind. In addition to market potential, the course of currency exchange rates and inflation rates in the important foreign markets play a central role in this decision process.

2. The Adjustment of Company Culture to the Special Aspects of International Activities

The dynamics of the world economy demand that companies involve themselves to an increasing extent in the various forms of foreign activity. This orientation towards increased foreign activity forces companies into internal and external processes of adjustment. The structures which have been handed down in matters of company organisation, personnel and finance can be harmonised with the new dimensions of foreign activity either not at all or only in a very restricted manner. In order to cope with the demands of international markets it is necessary to establish a new suitably adjusted form of organisation, an appropriate financial framework and an internationally oriented personnel policy, and to undertake adjustments in purchasing, in research and development policy and, of course, in marketing. Companies thus undergo a pronounced structural and functional change as foreign activities are extended. A profound change in company culture thereby ensues.

Previous experience would suggest that international large companies are best placed to implement this process of change and adjustment in their organisations. Building on long years of international experience and on a basis of the systematic preparation of decisions by staff departments, and with the aid of external company advisers, the large companies succeed relatively well in coping with this process of adjustment. Medium-sized companies often find themselves confronted here with a complex of problems, since international experience, qualified personnel and often too the readiness to adjust are missing.

In the area of **finance** one would in the light of this have to, for example, include the possibilities of the Euromarket in the financing of foreign trade, or cooperate with the West German Credit Bank for Reconstruction (Kreditanstalt für Wiederaufbau, or KfW) or the German Finance Company for Participation in Developing Countries (Deutsche Finanzierungsgesellschaft für Beteiligung in Entwicklungsländern, or DEG) when undertaking foreign investment. In every case very close contact must be maintained with the commercial banks concerned and the banks for their part must provide an adequate service of information and advice for the foreign business.

In the area of **purchasing** it is a matter of utilising the international opportunities. The foremost aim is to secure advantages over other competitors by means of an appropriate purchasing policy – whether this be through the utilisation of production elements which are otherwise not available, or not available at the same value, or through the financially advantageous purchase of elements of the same value. This holds true not just for raw materials[9], but also for ready-made goods and trade goods in both the consumer and the investment goods sectors. A necessary prerequisite for the exploitation of the international opportunities of purchase is a very well-functioning information system.

---

[9] Cf. on this point also Meissner, H. G., Sohn, K.-H. (Eds.), Internationales Rohstoffmarketing, Dortmund. 1981.

In **research and development** it is important for companies to keep the door open to international development and also to foster the conditions which will favour the creative efforts of their own workers in this area. Some German large companies have recently established contact with American universities, which they get to work on individual research projects for them. However, cooperation with research facilities in foreign countries is still in its infancy. In this matter it is to be expected that a stronger research union will be established at least within the European Community, and that it will also be used by companies.

In the context of **personnel** the dynamics of the world economy force many companies towards processes of adjustment in two different directions. On the one hand it is a question of orienting one's own personnel policy – from the selection of personnel through training to personnel planning – towards the changing demands made by foreign activities. On the other hand companies are also faced by the task of having recourse to the international work market. One therefore finds at management level in foreign companies a number of so called "expatriates", whose international experience and readiness to adjust make them successful workers for their companies. The nationally inbred tradition of many German industrial companies still bars a number of them from insight into the necessity of adjusting their personnel policy to international circumstances.[10] Foreign business cannot be successfully administered by persons who remain strongly bound to national norms, rules and business practices and who have been trained solely along these lines. The adjustment of the personnel policy of companies involves of necessity the promotion of the knowledge of foreign languages and cultures among those who work for the company. Culture is transmitted particularly through direct and personal contacts and also through the relevant language, and mastering the language of the host country is not just a matter of politeness or of the facilitation of communication but also an essential prerequisite of any serious attempt to understand the special culture of the foreign country.

The necessity of adjusting the company culture becomes particularly clear in the **sales sector**. The internationalisation of sales, which in the case of some large companies extends right up to globalisation, requires the alignment of the decisions of companies to the multitude of environmental conditions which a system of international marketing entails. Adjustments become necessary in the fields of product policy, pricing policy, communications policy and distribution policy, that is in all sections of the marketing mix. An orientation of companies towards the home market, with foreign business being regarded simply as a welcome and temporary bonus and without its

---

[10] Cf. on this point Dülfer, E. (Ed.), Personelle Aspekte im Internationalen Marketing, Berlin 1983.

being recognised as having strategic significance for the future of these companies, is no longer commercially defensible under the present market conditions of Germany and Europe. Companies in the USA are in a different position here, as the size of the American home market may stop many companies from seeing foreign business as either necessary or attractive. The export orientation of American industry is therefore much less pronounced than is the case with Europe and Japan, and this can also be seen in the considerably smaller American export quotas.

Adjustment demands of companies more than a merely passive reaction to pre-existing environmental conditions. What is required instead is the active development of strategies in order to be able to win, maintain and insofar as possible further extend a desirable position on the international markets. With nothing more than passive reaction to developments on the world market or to the strategies of companies of other countries (Japanese firms, for example), West German companies will not succeed in coming to grips with the new style and above all with the growing importance of the international division of labour which has come into existence in today's world. This demands of companies that they undertake a scrutiny of principles and especially of strategy with respect to active adjustment both internally in West Germany and externally on the various foreign markets.

The international division of labour has already reached a level which pressurises companies towards accommodation, demanding in the long term their re-alignment to the changing structures of the world economy and the adaptation of their internal structures to long-term change. This requires the development and implementation of concepts of Strategic International Marketing. The integrative function of marketing, which should influence and structure all other sub-areas of company management as a leitmotiv,[11] is taken over by Strategic International Marketing when it comes to the foreign activities of companies. Strategic International Marketing is therefore not just a reaction to changing conditions in the world economy and to the specific challenges of opportunities and risks which they represent for companies, but attains a formative and directive function for every internationally oriented company.

[11] On the concept of marketing as it is at present understood cf. for example Kotler, Ph., Marketing Management 4th edition, Englewood Cliffs, N.J. 1980 or the contribution by Hill W., Marketing, in: Tietz, B.(Ed.): Handwörterbuch der Absatzwirtschaft, Stuttgart 1974, Columns 1233–1247.

3. Structural Change as a Consequence of International Orientation

The dynamics of the world economy, in conjunction with an increase in foreign activity, have triggered far-reaching processes of internal structural change in many companies. Such a structural change, a process of fundamentally new orientation, is to companies what the process of sociocultural change has been to society. This structural change leads, in the case of companies which are oriented towards foreign trade, to a change in company philosophy, to a realignment of the goals which are derived from it and thus also in the means which the companies employ in order to attain these goals. The dominant trading patterns and models of the companies change under the presure of the increasing orientation towards the world market.

This structural change expresses itself most clearly in the fact that traditional production-dominated thinking, the exclusive orientation of industrial companies towards the area of marketing material goods, must be discarded in favour of an expanded service concept. This represents a structural change, which parallels the one triggered by the penetration of the marketing concept into company philosophy. In International Marketing this orientation towards service is intensified even further by the special aspects of foreign business.

It is true that the products and the standard of technology realised in them represent the basis for any international business, but they are not by themselves sufficient to build up a lasting foreign trade. It is precisely in the area of investment goods, which represent the real backbone of German exports, that the services which back up the supply of products, that is the software such as finance and training facilities, play a decisive role.[12] The comprehensive solution of a problem, which the foreign buyer expects of an overseas supplier, relates not just to the item itself, the product, but to an increasing extent to a **system**, in which the product of course plays an important part, but a part which is proportionately of ever-decreasing importance to the actual decisions being made concerning specific offers. In plant construction this growing emphasis on the importance of service for international business is becoming particularly clear, and this is a sector which fulfills a pilot function for German foreign trade, owing not just to the economic but also to the political and social significance of the individual projects concerned, such as mines, power stations, chemical plants or infrastructural projects such as port and road construction.

---

[12] Cf: Backhaus, K., Investitionsgüter-Marketing, Munich 1982, pp. 105 ff.

This development demands that companies change their priorities, which have up to now guided traditional company philosophy with an orientation towards the home market and technological efficiency. This also makes necessary a corresponding organisational restructuring in companies which operate on the international level.

The other profound structural change relates to the change in the conception of the market. Industrial development was borne by a **home market concept**. Whenever the markets in the home countries became too small, states and governments worked together with companies to extend this concept of the home market to other countries – until the beginning of the present century this was done mainly by the establishment and expansion of colonies.

The road to a new understanding of partnership in the world economy was first opened by the political developments which followed upon the end of the Second World War and which led to the independence of those territories which were previously dependent upon the European colonial powers. And so it holds true for German industry that only prospering countries with progressive economies can be good customers in the long run, whereas economic crises and destabilisation on foreign markets adversely affect the possibilities of supply from Germany. The converse is equally true; only an economically sound and growing West Germany can offer market outlets and opportunities to the developing and threshold countries. This consciousness of the economic unity of the world is today much more clearly marked than has ever been the case previously in the history of the world economy. A greater awareness of the change which has taken place is to be found among the companies of West Germany than those of former colonial powers or the present-day superpowers. As a consequence the West German economy has been more successful in adjusting to this new constellation. This aspect too of structural change has had organisational consequences for companies oriented towards foreign trade, in the manner for example in which they allow their foreign partner firms or affiliates a greater degree of autonomy. This is in order to avoid any colonial or imperialistic pretensions which would, in any case, given the current situation of the development and differentiation of the world economy, be more likely to lead to failure than to the construction of a stable foreign business relationship.

This structural change brought about by foreign activity is linked both for companies and for business management theory, to a paradigm change in the sense employed by Thomas Kuhn[13] in his account of scientific revolutions. Companies need to understand this paradigm, work upon it, assimilate it and employ it strategically. Strategic International Marketing therefore represents

[13] Cf. Kuhn, TT.. The Structure of Scientific Revolutions, 2nd Edn., Chicago 1970.

a particularly clear paradigm change both in the economic sciences and in the practice of company management.

4. Concentration Processes and the Development of Multinational Companies

Foreign activities have become a major factor in the growth of companies and the formation of combines. Foreign activities are therefore also always related to processes of concentration in the economy. Yet the causal connection between foreign activities and the formation of combines has not up to now been examined systematically by researchers in the field of either political economy or business management. Therefore one can at present only verify the phenomenon that it is the large national, and above all the international firms, which have had a particularly large share in the development of the world economy and of world trade.

In saying this it is extremely difficult to decide whether companies succeeded in attaining their size and their rise to international significance by forcing their foreign activities, or whether the size they had already attained more or less forced them into an awareness of the international market opportunities. Here too there is a lack of empirically reliable research which would clearly demonstrate the connection between foreign activities and the concentration of the attentions of companies.

We are therefore taking as our starting-point that we are dealing with a two-way process, such as is typical of complex developments: foreign activities provide companies with the possibility of increasing their turnover, utilising their capacity and distributing their fixed costs more efficiently – and thus improving their profitability. Improved profitability is in turn the prerequisite for the expansion of research and development, production capacity and marketing activities (Diagram 8).

The position on the world market, once attained, provides companies with the opportunities of developing a strategy for combines which leads ultimately to the formation of multinational companies.

What happens in the world economy is clearly influenced by the existence of **multinational companies**. The term refers to those companies which have fundamentally geared their company philosophy towards the world market as a whole, without allowing themselves to be restricted by the existing national borders.

Multinational companies are such firms as no longer restrict themselves in principle to a national framework, but follow an international concept with

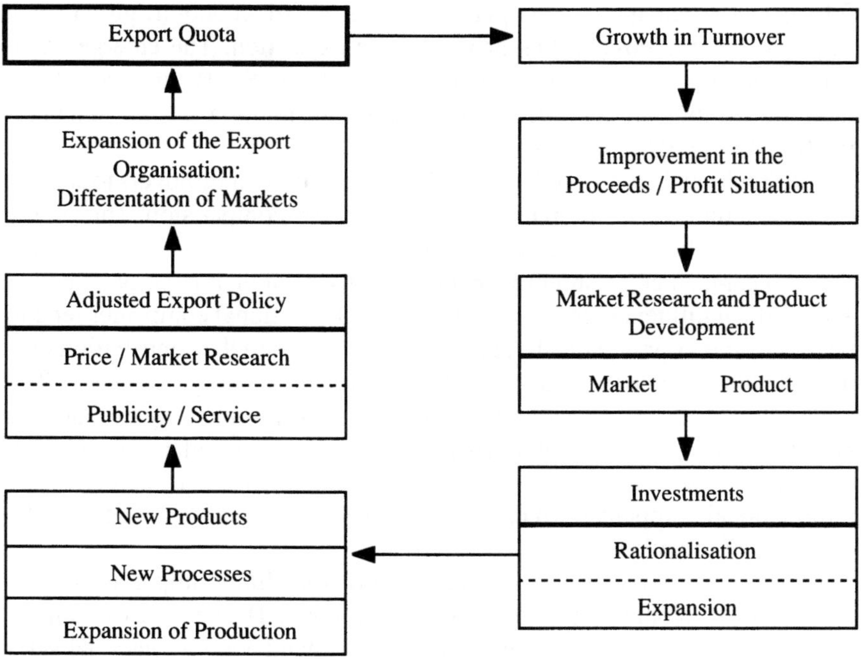

Diagram 8. The connections between export quota and company growth.[14]

respect to policies in the areas of sales, purchase, investment and finance. The transition from a national to a multinational enterprise cannot be determined with pinpoint precision. But a company is taken to be multinational when it makes more than 25% of its investments in foreign markets and this in more than 5 different countries.[15]

The emergence of multinational or transnational companies represents a special development in the present world economy. With the development of these multinational companies it becomes clear that the existing national borders are too narrow for the possibilities and necessities of economic development. The national states arose in their present form and basic ideology in the pre-industrial period. They served to secure the political and cultural unity of individual nationalities and were to this extent a necessary prerequisite for the impressive economic development and the blossoming trade of the Industrial Revolution. But at the present time national states cannot

[14] Taken from: Meissner, H. G., Exportpolitik vom Standpunkt der Unternehmensführung, Herne and Berlin 1974, p. 15.
[15] Cf. Sieber, E., Die internationale Unternehmung, in: Engeleiter, H.-J. (Ed.), Gegenwartsfragen der Unternehmensführung, Herne and Berlin 1966, pp.51–68.

fully meet the demands made by companies as regards economic growth and, in particular, the possibilities of worldwide expansion. The emergence of superstructures, such as are seen in the U.S.A., the U.S.S.R., and the E.C., is therefore the logical consequence of the increasing importance of business for the future of peoples.

Multinational companies can develop the size of their turnovers to such an extent that the budgets of many states are small by comparision. The United Nations have therefore taken an increasing interest in the activities of multinational companies, in order to prevent any misuse of their position of power and political influence. In the meantime the multinational companies tend to be judged rather pragmatically, and then with regard to the contribution they make to other countries, especially the group of developing countries.[16] The multinational companies represent the most effective form of organisation for bringing about an international transfer of capital and particularly of technical know-how and management methods. To this extent it is precisely the multinational companies which have become the "agents of change" in the economy of today's world.

The multinational companies have a correspondingly important role to play in the development of International Marketing. The necessity of adjustment to local production conditions on the one hand and international sales opportunities on the other has forced multinational companies above everyone else to come to grips with and give shape to the central theme of International Marketing, namely that of unification versus differentiation. The great financial possibilities of multinational companies and the broad product palette which many of these companies can offer, have made these companies the vanguard of International Marketing.[17] Worldwide marketing plans, based on systematically conducted market research, have been developed by the multinational companies. Pricing and product strategies have been supported by the possibilities of transfer pricing, and cooperation with internationally active advertising agencies has made it possible for multinational companies in particular to develop worldwide publicity and image strategies. One may cite as example here the worldwide business policy of IBM, which became not just the pacesetter in computer technology, but also played no small part in the development of International Marketing.

---

[16] Cf. Pausenberger, E., Internationale Unternehmungen in Entwicklungsländern, Düsseldorf and Vienna 1980, pp. 43ff.

[17] Cf. Keegan, W. J., Multinational Marketing Management, Englewood Cliffs/N.J. 1974.

5. The Internationalisation of Medium-Sized Companies

The dynamics of the world economy have led to a situation where it is not solely the multinational companies or the important international combines which profit from the opportunities offered by the international divisions of labour, but where inclusion in the worldwide network of trade has become an important competitive factor for medium-sized companies as well.[18] At any rate it is medium-sized companies which encounter specific difficulties when establishing or expanding foreign operations, and these difficulties arise particularly in connection with their low capital cover and their insufficient personnel resources. Governments, official bodies and associations therefore attempt to improve the market position of medium-sized companies involved in foreign trade by means of information services, credit assistance and advisory service.[19] The aid given to medium-sized companies is essentially concentrated in the area of export advice and the promotion of foreign investments.[20]

Now that medium-sized firms as well are increasingly subject to internationalisation, it is precisely these firms that will undergo far-reaching processes of adjustment, in order both to iron out their weaknesses in international business and further to expand their existing strengths. A major strength of medium-sized firms in international business lies in their flexibility in dealing with even the very special requests of foreign customers. It is medium-sized companies above all which can offer individual problem-solving to foreign customers. International combines on the other hand are only able and willing to offer such individualised service in exceptional circumstances and then only in connection with large orders. A further strength of medium-sized companies in international business is to be found in the very personal and informal manner of communication with the foreign trading partner or customer. The cultural and also the political and ideological barriers to world trade can be overcome more easily by this form of personal communication than by an impersonal and formal organisation of foreign trade.

The problem areas with the internationalisation of medium-sized companies may be considered primarily under three aspects. Firstly, the **financial resources** of medium-sized companies are usually narrowly restricted and allow little room for manoeuvre for strategically necessary investments in

[18] Cf. Steinmann, H., Kumar, B., Wasner, A., Die Internationalisierung von Mittelbetrieben, Wiesbaden 1977, and the contributions of various authors in BFuP, No. 6, 1985.

[19] Cf. Vogt, V., System der Exportförderung in der Bundesrepublik Deutschland, in: Stahr, G. (Ed.), Exportpraxis – Handbuch für den deutschen Exporteur, A VIII.

[20] Cf. Börgers, K.-H., Quambusch, L., Export und Auslandsinvestitionen, Cologne 1985.

foreign markets. A certain amount of help may be provided here by state support schemes for foreign trade, and also by closer cooperation with the company's bank, but above all by an expansion of the company's own capital by an enlargement of the circle of shareholders. However the latter alternative in particular often comes to grief on the directorship and ownership structures of medium-sized companies, so a large number of interesting foreign deals are not realised through fear of dilution of the firm by the addition of non-family members to its board.

The second aspect relates to the demands made of the **leadership and organisational structure** of an internationally active company, demands which are often not adequately met. Medium-sized companies are primarily family companies, so that all important (and sometimes too the unimportant) decisions are made by one person or by a very small circle of persons, and this is linked to an organisational structure which is strictly hierarchical. In such cases the problems lie both in a form of organisation which is inadequate to the needs of a company which is growing and internationally active, and in the wasted potential of colleagues who are themselves capable of assuming leadership roles.

The third problem field in the internationalisation of medium-sized companies is likewise rooted in the leadership and organisational structure of these companies and expresses itself in the **attitude of mind** which seeks to maintain old and proven patterns of decision for as long as possible. Bound by tradition and overburdened by daily business, many owners of medium-sized companies fail to come to grips either innovatively or strategically with the possible future development of their firm, so that a large number of opportunities on international markets are either not noticed or neglected.

Therefore it is not least in the area of marketing that medium-sized firms will feel the pressure towards adaptation in international business. Many medium-sized firms do not avail of a consciously planned marketing policy, but adapt themselves in an ad hoc manner to any business opportunities which arise, for example at trade fairs.

Nevertheless the rising export quotas of medium sized-companies and their resultant increasing dependence on foreign trade makes it imperative that they develop concepts of Strategic International Marketing, as international combines and multinational companies have been doing for a number of years. In view of their limited resources medium-sized companies must form a clear picture of what foreign markets they want to concentrate on and with what products, of how they estimate the future of these markets and with what strategies they wish to secure and expand their position on these markets.

To this extent Strategic International Marketing also becomes an appropriate task for medium-sized companies. The future of many medium-sized companies will depend on their ability to utilise the concepts and instruments of International Marketing in order to establish and then further extend their positions on the various foreign markets.

6. The International Culture of Companies

In the course of their existence all companies develop a quite definite and distinctive "culture". The term is used to describe the system of values which informs the dealings and modes of behaviour of a company. The prevailing system of values of a company determines the courses of action open to it in making specific decisions.[21]

In the context of companies increasing their foreign activities it is important for them to develop a specific **international culture**. The traditional company culture of German firms consists largely in a technically oriented culture. Technical efficiency and the securing of the qualitative level of production represented the dominant ideals towards which all other company aims were directed. In addition, traditional company culture is hall-marked by organisational and personal ideals. Some companies develop a pronounced hierarchical culture: the organisation becomes the ideal to which everything else is subordinate, leading even to the development of bureaucratic superstructures such as were created in German industrial combines between the world wars. Other companies have developed a culture marked by centralisation around individual leading personalities – right up to the personality cult. In these cases the leading figure of the firm owner, or of a member of the board of directors, influences the decision processes of the company to a disproportionate extent, and this is a hindrance to coping with problems or with reality.

A prerequisite for successful activity on international markets is that companies become aware of the significance of their international culture and embed this culture as a positive force in their overall organisation and take appropriate account of it in their information, structuring and decision procedures. A conscious structuring of company culture can be built upon the following steps:[22]

---

[21] Cf. Byars, L. L., Strategic Management: Planning and Implementation, Concepts and Cases, New York 1984, p. 67.

[22] Cf. Marr, R., Problemaspekte bei der Entwicklung eines Wissenschaftsprogramms des "Internationalen Management" – aus personalwirtschaftlicher Sicht, in: Dülfer, E. (Ed.), Personelle Aspekte im Internationalen Management, Berlin 1983, p. 35.

- identification of the culture which is suited and appropriate to the existential requirements of the company;
- determination of the previously dominant culture in the company;
- identification of the deficits between the existing company culture and the one which is required;
- decisions about the methods to be employed to eliminate the deficits which have been registered;
- implementation of the company culture wished for and required by strategic concepts;
- repetition of this process, in order to guarantee the adjustment of the company culture to the changing environment.

The elements of the international culture necessary for companies consist above all in their becoming open to international market opportunities and at the same time becoming aware of the risks which their international involvements entail. Openness towards the variety of international market opportunities is of central significance here. This must become the guiding principle of the culture of every internationally active company, to which all other aspects such as personnel planning or the procurement of capital are subordinated. The international culture of companies requires a consistent orientation towards service as well as a readiness to work together with foreign colleagues, traders, investors and consumers. There arises thereby a new international team spirit which is the precondition for the economic success and the long-term securing of international markets.

The international culture of companies also absolutely requires an adjustment of personnel policy. Here the companies must achieve a much greater degree of mobility and planned development of their personnel resources than has been the case with the technological or the person-oriented company culture. The workers must be prepared systematically, comprehensively and in good time for foreign tasks, and cultural conflict connected with foreign activity is not the least of the items to be kept in mind here. Furthermore, career opportunities must be kept open in the home country for any workers who have spent a number of years in the company's service abroad.

Just as with the personnel planning aspect of matters, decisions concerning financial planning must also be made within the framework of the prevailing value system of the international company culture. Multinational companies and international combines have long since taken steps to meet this requirement, for example by the introduction of financial holdings. The increase in foreign trade activities must now force many more companies – including those of the medium-sized sector – to make their financial arrangements in an international setting. This then entails the countering of currency and transfer risks by the development of appropriate strategies of risk elimination and risk limitation.[23]

The international culture of companies enfolds itself especially in the area of the market orientation of companies. For the companies it is a matter of seeing the possibilities which open up on international markets not just as additional or complementary opportunities, but as existential necessities for the securing of turnover, growth, profitability, employment, research capacity, for the opening of market potential and for the long-term existence of the company.

The area of International Marketing and particularly activity in Strategic International Marketing therefore represent the real focus of the international culture of companies. It is International Marketing which shows whether a company has assimilated this international culture and thus made it into the guiding maxim of its existence, or whether the international activities are nothing more than chance events which have no real effect on the existence of the company.

---

[23] Cf. Pausenberger, E., Völker, H., Praxis des internationalen Finanzmanagement: eine empirische Untersuchung von Finanzierung, Kapitalstrukturgestaltung und Cash Management in internationalen Unternehmen, Wiesbaden 1985; Hielscher, U., Instrumente zur Begrenzung von Währungsrisiken, in: BFuP, Vol. 37, No. 6 (Nov.1985), pp. 531–548.

E. Concepts of Marketing in Foreign Trade

1. Processes of Development towards International Marketing

International Marketing is simultaneously a specialisation and a further development of the general concept of marketing, and for international marketing too the decisive starting-point is the **principle of interaction**.

It is precisely through this principle of interaction that the marketing concept distinguishes itself from traditional sales theory, such as was developed in German business management theory by Erich Gutenberg in particular.[1] In the marketing concept the traditional processes of the exchange of goods, services and money are made dependent variables of both pre – and post – introduced processes of communication. The communication spoken of here is of two types; firstly the information required by the companies about the expectations, attitudes and motives of consumers or investors, and which is obtained by the instruments of market research and futurology, and, secondly, the information directed towards consumers or investors about the performance and supply potentials of companies, and this is transmitted primarily by means of publicity.

The further development from nationally oriented to International Marketing thus requires market research and publicity to extend to the particularities of buyer and investor behaviour in various cultural environments. This results in specialisation in the marketing decisions specific to each foreign market. Foreign market research must therefore be undertaken in a manner which is especially careful and culturally adjusted – insofar as possible it should be carried out by a local market research institute, in order to avoid, or at least be able to reduce, any prejudices or lack of sensitivity towards the problems of a foreign market which might exist even at the pre-decision stage. In the same way specialisation in International Marketing extends to the particularities of

[1] Cf. Gutenberg, E., Grundlagen der Betriebswirtschaftslehre, Vol. 2, Der Absatz, 17th. Edn., Heidelberg 1984.

all other marketing functions and instruments, from product design to the choice of channels of distribution to advertising in foreign countries.[2]

The further development of the general marketing concept within the framework of International Marketing consists especially in the fact that the overall service aspect receives a new quality. In the context of the modern marketing concepts, there occurs with a large number of export products not just a relativisation of the price as a marketing instrument, but also a relativisation of the product in the sense of hardware. The decision to buy is swayed in many instances by the services which are offered to foreign customers along with the product, and these encompass problem-solving in all spheres from the technical to the financial to the field of personnel.

The internationalisation of the marketing concept requires the **pluralisation of the decision horizon** of companies. It is no longer a question of one single market, but of a variety of international markets and market segments. This pluralisation requires internationally active companies to come up with a new and suitably adjusted strategic concept, particularly with reference to risk elimination and to the securing of future market opportunities.

Finally, International Marketing must lead to a consistent humanisation of marketing: proper regard for the sociocultural framework makes companies meet their partners on the world market with more understanding and with greater human openness. It is precisely through International Marketing that the partner-oriented basic model of foreign trade comes into being.

The development towards International Marketing corresponds to the processes of increasing orientation of the individual companies towards the world economy. It is a matter of economic history that right up to the years which followed the end of the Second World War German companies were bound into the world economy through trading houses which were based in the Hanseatic cities or in other places with international connections. Foreign trade activities were reduced to export and import deals, complemented by transport and insurance arrangements and the corresponding financial transactions.[3] The actual manufacturer of goods did not come into direct contact with the foreign importer, and certainly not into any with the foreign user. For the producer it was like a deal completed on the home market just like any other, except that certain regulations concerning packaging and trade descriptions had to be taken into account. The foreign business matters were handled exclusively by the trading house.

As industry developed, this form of indirect foreign trade was superseded by direct foreign trade, which involves direct contact between the manufactu-

---

[2] Cf. Meissner, H. G., Probleme der internationalen Werbung im Überblick, in: Tietz, B. (Ed.), Die Werbung, Vol. 3, Landsberg am Lech 1982, pp. 3018–3043.

[3] Cf. Ohling, H., Export – Import – Spedition, 7th Edn., Wiesbaden 1973, pp. 21.ff.

rer in one country and the importer or consumer in another. The greater the share of investment goods in the export range becomes, and the more complex the technology exported and the more explanation it requires, the more direct contact, with its opportunities for problem-specific dialogue, becomes essential to the acquisitive potential of the exporting industrial company. In connection with this development it is noteworthy that the traditional trading houses have undergone extensive weeding-out processes as they were in large measure driven from their special position in the world economy, and in the meantime have come to form only a limited segment of the foreign trade market, whose importance is restricted to special branches of trade or special regions of the world.

The reshuffling of the export range in favour of complex investment goods, up to and including large-scale plant construction, and the growth in the volume of exports have led in a further step to the necessity for spare part warehouses, service stations and training centres. On the basis of these first investments in foreign markets, assembly plants have subsequently been set up, frequently at the insistence of the importing countries who hope by this means to save foreign exchange and to create additional work-places, with corresponding technical and commercial know-how, for their own citizens. These assemblies are carried out at a level appropriate to the technological standard of the country concerned and to available production capacities, while product completion is gradually extended towards further levels of sophistication. The end-point of this development is the setting-up of production companies abroad, either as affiliates or as joint ventures. In fact joint venture formation[4] is in the meantime demanded by many developing countries as a precondition for the approval of the investments of foreign companies, in order both to prevent the alienation of local business and to establish a connection to the international development of technological know-how and management skill.

If, as a result of repeated foundations and participations in various markets, a company is linked to a whole series of affiliates or joint ventures abroad, then it completes the transition to international company. Under this heading two different types of internationally active company have established themselves in the world economy, and these are firstly the national or international combines and secondly the multinational or transnational companies. In the case of the national or international companies one is dealing with combines which still display a national identity as, for example, a German or a French company, while at the same time developing activities of a more or less international character, which can reach a point where the turnover in the home

[4] Cf. Meissner, H. G., Joint Ventures, in: Büschgen, H. E. (Ed.) Handwörterbuch der Finanzwissenschaft, Stuttgart 1976, Col. 917–924.

country is smaller than the export turnover and the turnover of the foreign associated and affiliated companies. What is decisive here is the identification of the company with a national state, which leads to the headquarters of the combine being maintained in the home country, although in a number of cases a holding company is interposed and the seat of the latter is chosen with a view to matters of taxation and finance.

With multinational companies on the other hand the question of national identity is relativised. Multinational companies make their decisions of world-wide scope with a view to the best production conditions, the most far-reaching tax advantages and possibilities of finance, or the most promising markets which they can find among the offers which countries make them. National frontiers represent to the multinational companies obstacles to their potential development, so that they strive to avoid these hindrances or at least keep them as low as possible. This procedure would seem sensible according to purely economic criteria of decision, but it has drawn the fire of international criticism onto the multinational companies, and the United Nations have joined in the attack. A code of behaviour for multinational companies was therefore drawn up on the basis of the discussion before the United Nations[5], with the intention of integrating the multinational companies into the existing world political order with as little conflict as possible. In this manner the precedence is meant to be established of the decisions of politicians oriented towards national states over those of managers oriented towards the whole world.

In the case of indirect foreign trade the market orientation takes the form primarily of traditional sales policy. The buyers can in these circumstances merely react to the activities of the companies. The area of direct foreign trade is characterised by an effective interactive process between producers and foreign users. The basis of many international contacts and foreign trade successes is personal communication, such as takes place particularly at foreign trade fairs and international specialist exhibitions, or within the context of travel by leading executives, with visits paid to important foreign customers.

Systematically conducted market research, taken for granted on the home market, has up to now only been practised in exceptional cases in this other context. The strong personalisation of communication in foreign business has however also led to companies not just concentrating on their abilities to solve problems of a purely technical nature, but also being stimulated to develop their own problem-solving capacities in other areas through confrontation

[5] Cf. Tiewul, S.A.,.The General and Political Principles of Behavior in the United Nations Code on Conduct of Transnational Corporations, in: Wacker, W., Haussmann, H., Kumar, B. (Eds.), Internationale Unternehmensführung,.Berlin 1981, pp. 351–377.

with the additional problems of the customer. Of course technical efficiency is now as always a very significant marketing instrument, but it is being complemented to an increasing degree by other problem-solving capabilities in the spheres of finance, personnel and organisation.

Such a change in foreign business dealings is accompanied by the first steps towards International Marketing. This is not, of course, to say that an attitude already prevails that all decision processes within the companies must be subordinated to the prior claims of any orientation towards International Marketing. This does not arise in any systematic or consistent manner until one comes to the international firms – or where it is even more prominent – to the multinational ones. The marketing successes of the international companies have in the meantime led, just as has the increasing significance of marketing in home markets, to the concept of marketing radiating outwards towards a range of medium-sized companies.

The further development of International Marketing is therefore doubly stimulated: both by the example which emanates from the internationally active combines, and by the transfer of marketing concepts from activities in the home market. Marketing on the home market has developed particularly in the area of consumer goods, whereas it is only in recent years that its application to the fields of investment goods and services has come to be discussed and used on a deeper level.

2. Aspects of the Design of International Transfer Processes

a) The Processing of Foreign Deals

The utilisation of international market opportunities is not possible without a mastery of the techniques of foreign trade. What is at issue here is the design of international transfer processes between companies and organisations. The processing of foreign trade deals can be sub-divided into various phases and is for the most part subject to a scheme which can be clarified by means of the following:[6]

1) Preparing the way for business
   (Opening the market and acquisition),

[6] Cf. on this point also the extensive presentation in Meissner, H. G., Außenhandels-Marketing, Stuttgart 1981, pp. 122–127.

2) Planning the offer
   (Usually in response to a customer's request),
3) Drawing up the contract
   (Setting-down of performance and consideration as well as agreement on trade clauses – INCOTERMS),
4) Carrying out the contract
   (Making ready the goods ordered, by production or by purchase),
5) Arrangement of transport
   (Type of transport, insurance, customs papers, etc.),
6) Settlement of payment
   (Payment conditions, letters of credit, etc.),
7) Medium and long-term financing of exports,
8) Guarantees and warranties,
9) Subsequent contact and follow-up deals.

b) State Support Measures

The specific transfer potential of companies in the context of International Marketing also consists in obtaining and integrating state assistance and support into foreign trade activities. Such state assistance exists firstly in the home countries of the companies (in West Germany as well as in other industrial countries), and there are also similar measures for the promotion of foreign trade in force in the target countries. In addition to this supranational organisations such as the EC and international institutions such as the United Nations promote foreign trade indirectly.

West Germany has developed a system of state support for the foreign trade activities of companies which is geared towards the market economy.[7] The support measures relate to support both for the export of goods and for direct investments abroad. The "classical" support measures in the export of goods are the supply of information, rebates of value added tax which has already been levied (tax concession at borders), export finance, export credit insurance and exchange rate insurance.

In the case of direct investments abroad the support also takes the form of special policies for risks, such as the agreeing of contracts for investment support and the West German government's undertaking of guarantees for capital investment in developing countries and state trade countries. There is also support for the financing of investment, and this is effected in West Germany through the Credit Bank for Reconstruction (Kreditanstalt für Wiederaufbau – KFW) and the German Finance Corporation for Participation

[7] Cf. Berekoven, L., Internationales Marketing, 2nd. Edn., Herne and Berlin 1985, pp. 231 ff.

in Developing Countries (Deutsche Finanzierungsgesellschaft für Beteiligungen in Entwicklungsländern – DEG).

The West German state makes its main contribution to the trade-political support of German foreign business through the provision of information, and this is carried out by the Federal Office for Foreign Trade Information (Bundesstelle für Außenhandelsinformation – BfAi) in Cologne. The BfAi has developed into a centre for the procurement and distribution of foreign trade information in West Germany. The BfAi strives constantly to adjust its supply of information to the ever-changing requirements of German industry. For this task it makes increasing use of automated data processing to make its information available as quickly and as comprehensively as possible to interested parties in companies, but also to those in associations, chambers of commerce, academic life and others whom it may concern, such as foreign trade advisers and engineering consultants.[8]

In planning the International Marketing of companies it is becoming increasingly important to integrate the state promotional programmes both at home and abroad into decision-making. This requires of companies a quite different attitude to International Marketing than to marketing decisions which relate only to the home market. The state promotional measures exert a noticeable pressure towards adjustment on the companies. Companies must make a specific management effort to acquaint themselves with the opportunities available for support, and in view of the complexity and variety of state support measures for foreign trade they must see to the creation of an appropriate department with competent workers.

c) The Risks of Foreign Trade

The techniques of foreign trade have been evolved largely as a result of dealing with the typical risks of foreign trade. These risks have their roots in the basic configuration of foreign trade, in that the trading partners live under different economic and legal systems, and in that there are frequently considerable periods of time between the dispatch of the goods from the exporting country, their arrival in the importing country and the corresponding payment procedures, and these periods must be bridged by a specific risk-management policy.

The foreign trade risks and also the possibilities of coping with these risks exhibit a complex structure which is illustrated in Diagram 9.

---

[8] Cf. Bundesstelle für Außenhandelsinformation (BfAi)(Ed.), Informationsbedarf und Informationsverhalten ausgewählter Wirtschaftszweige bezüglich außenwirtschaftlicher Informationen, Cologne 1985.

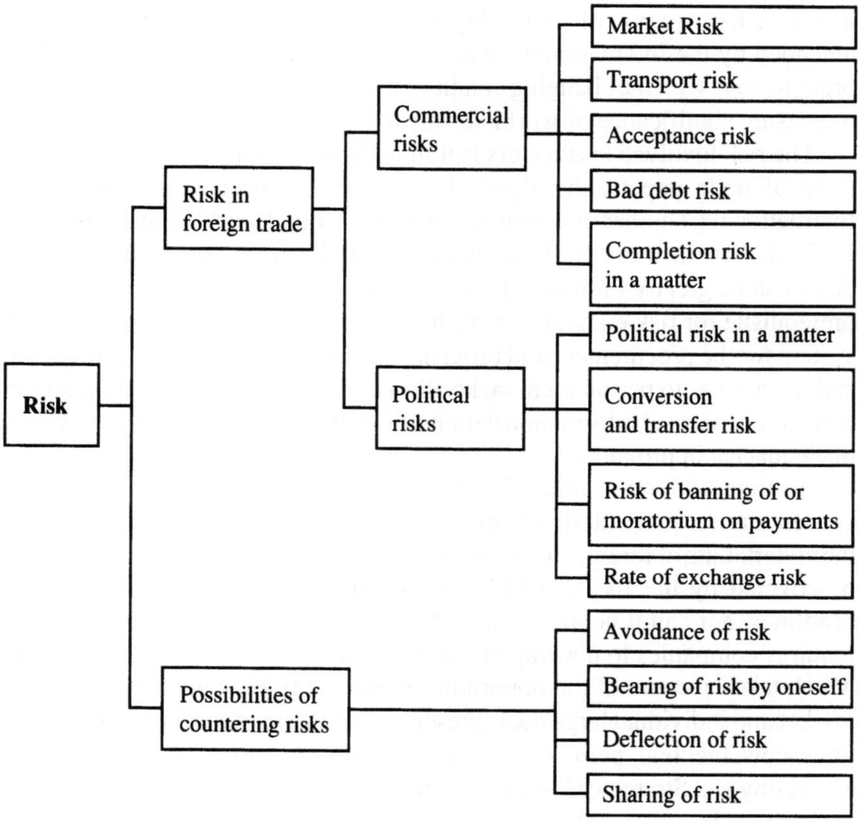

Diagram 9. The structure of foreign trade risks [9]

The commercial risk can be limited by the wording of the contract. Particularly useful here are the internationally recognised trading stipulations which were first drawn up in 1936 by the International Chamber of Commerce, the INCOTERMS. These specify in their various regulations the rights and duties of importer and exporter, and set down the place and time at which the costs and risks are transferred from the exporter to the importer. The contractual agreements most frequently entered into for risk transfer are the:

FOB clauses (for exports)
and the
CIF clauses (for imports),

[9] Diagram taken from Topritzhofer, E., Moser, R., Das Exportgeschäft, 2nd. Edn., Vienna 1984, p. 6.

and in each case a port of dispatch or of entry is named.[10] The Incoterms were amended by the International Chamber of Commerce in 1953 and 1974, in order to cope with the changing conditions in the world economy and with the increasing significance of world air traffic.

The risk involved in transfers is limited by the guidelines for the encashment of trade papers; these guidelines have also been drawn up by the International Chamber of Commerce and have found worldwide acceptance.

With these instruments the economic and political risks of foreign business deals can be greatly limited or reduced to an acceptable level. An important prerequisite for risk management is that companies have available to them a system for the procurement and provision of information of sufficient quality and quantity as to permit them make allowances for the risks of foreign trade under the aspects of information deficits, difficulties in analysis and, above all, inadequacies in prognosis.

A strategic foreign trade risk in the sense of a threat to a company's existence arises particularly in connection with long-term supply deals or with the undertaking of foreign investments. This strategic foreign trade risk cannot be covered by the INCOTERMS or by deals involving foreign currency deadlines, nor can it be met by any state cushion against risks, but rather it requires companies to develop an internationally oriented strategic concept which takes account of the opportunities and the risks which the individual market and individual large deals present to the future of the companies. This represents the real point of intersection between Strategic International Marketing and Strategic Company Management. This results in the necessity of Strategic International Marketing for these companies which are oriented towards foreign trade.

The greater the importance of an international involvement for a company (with regard to the period of time foreseen and the extent to which company resources will be bound up), whether this occurs in the form of foreign investment or in other forms of cooperation in foreign trade, the greater the importance of strategic considerations becomes. Many companies only grow into this existential dimension of international involvement as their economic expansion gets under way, so that before this happens they have only a small fund of experience on which to draw when they are actually making their decisions.

[10] See for further discussion of this point: Meissner, H. G., Außenhandels-Marketing, Stuttgart 1981, pp. 92–95.

d) Systems Selling

The particular importance and the significance of transfer processes in foreign trade emerge most clearly with Systems Selling, which represents an essential form of sales deal in large plant construction.[11] By systems selling is meant the international distribution of complex systems, by contrast with the traditional component-based export trade. These systems consist of a comprehensive supply programme of hardware and software, which is today often only possible in a manner which provides proper goods and performance if several companies, sometimes from a number of different countries, cooperate. In these cases the handling of the business is normally given over to a general contractor, who is a contractual partner of the foreign customer. His task is to assemble the relevant tender and to organise the process of purchase and production, as well as delivery, assembly and test-run.

A second important component included in the package is the financing of such a systems project. In the matter of financing, various sources of finance are combined in such a way with respect to deadlines, interest rates and sureties that the project concerned obtains an optimum financial structure. In particular there occurs a mixture of financing from both the manufacturer and the buyer, and national, supranational and international sources of finance are taken into consideration. The organisation and the techniques of financing in the plant construction sector are referred to as "financial engineering"[12] and have an important part to play as a marketing instrument in international business.

A further important aspect of systems selling is that the product offered includes not just hardware, but also software. When the deal is closed on the supply of hardware and its financing, an agreement is also made concerning the appropriate formation and training for the personnel of the foreign customer, in order to be able to run the plant as efficiently as possible. It has in the meantime come to be taken for granted that tenders for the supply of complex plants to developing and threshold countries will contain elements offering training. This training takes place either on the spot (sometimes as initiation into the use of plant which has already been constructed) or is undertaken at the home-bases of the companies or in appropriate training institutes in the exporting country.[13]

---

[11] Cf. on this point Engelhard, W. H., Laßmann, G. (Eds.), Anlagen-Marketing, in: ZfbF, 1977, special supplement No. 7.

[12] Cf. on this point Backhaus, K., Auftragsplanung im industriellen Anlagengeschäft, Stuttgart 1980, pp. 222 ff.

[13] Cf. Carl-Duisberg Centren (Eds.), Ausbildungsangebote der deutschen Wirtschaft für Entwicklungsländer, Cologne 1984.

In addition to training personnel to operate plant which has been supplied, general marketing and management techniques must also be transmitted within the framework of systems selling. This training and transfer aspect of international business makes its own very special contribution to the further integration of the world economy. The experiences of the West German Carl Duisberg Gesellschaft have made it clear that offers to supply training both at home and abroad are not the exclusive preserve of international combines, but that medium-sized engineering firms are also making increasing use of this instrument in order to confirm and expand their position on the international market. An interesting development in this regard is the joint training board which has been set up by the German printing machine industry, and which has managed to establish its own training centre in Singapore.[14]

3. The Temporal Horizon of International Marketing Decisions

In international business too, the classification of decisions into short-, medium- and long-term ones is quite important. **Short-term decisions** (with a horizon of up to one year) may relate, say, to individual decisions on pricing or communications policy, and may deal with matters such as the granting of a reduction or participation in a foreign trade fair. In many cases state trade countries make it a condition of granting a contract that the company concerned also takes part in the trade fairs of the country. When negotiating with a buying organisation in a state trade country over a contract which is very important for a company, participation in a trade fair in that country is essential.

Medium-term decisions (planning horizon between one and five years) in International Marketing relate to the choice of an advertising agency, the choice of distribution channels and representation abroad, for example the question as to whether the company will set up its own distribution organisation or whether it will work with independent commercial representatives. Its own distribution organisation ensures better contact with the parent company and leads to the image of the company being impressed more deeply in the consciousness of the customer. On the other hand independent representation has cost advantages and ensures an intimate knowlege of the market in the relevant foreign country. The decision concerning the form of distribution on foreign markets thus depends on a variety of factors. And once it is is taken,

---

[14] Cf. Print Promotion Programm der Druckmaschinenindustrie im VDMA.

it can only be revised with difficulty. A decision about distribution leaves a company committed to a specific distribution system for a period of years.

It is the **long-term decisions** (planning horizon of more than five years) which are of decisive importance for International Marketing. Long-term decisions establish the basic structure of the activities of companies and can only be revised in exceptional cases and at great transactional cost. An example of the long-term decision would be one to achieve a certain volume of turnover and thereby a certain share of a foreign market. This long-term decision of principle then requires a whole range of medium- and short-term decisions to adapt it to concrete configurations of the market and to the competition on the market concerned.

The long-term aspect of the decision is related to the product and performance programme which is to be offered on the specific market. This also includes a partial adjustment of the products to the local conditions, for example the technical finish of motor vehicles so that they conform to local exhaust regulations and other technical norms prescribed for road traffic. The long-term aspect also relates to the choice of strategy which will be brought to bear upon a specific foreign market. A decision about involvement in a foreign market must be coupled with one about long-term strategy which will be used to open up and to operate upon that market. Once chosen this strategy must be adhered to for as long as possible and can only be altered for the most pressing reasons, such as avoiding a loss of image to the company concerned. It must also be noted that certain objective grounds (for example, ones of a legal nature) can prevent or hinder a change and furthermore, not the least important aspect of the matter to be borne in mind is that long-term decisions are in many cases linked to extensive investment and thereby tie down resources, so that if wrong decisions are made there can be considerable consequences for the success of the company.

Although publicity is rarely discussed under aspects of company strategy, it must be realised in the case of International Marketing that the fixing of the advertising style introduces long-term accents, which can then only be changed or corrected with extreme difficulty. In general it may be stated that all decisions which relate to the **image** of a company obtain a special significance in the context of the long-term planning of the company on foreign markets. Foreign companies above all must adopt a highly sensitive image strategy. In addition they are directly identified with the national image of their country of origin (e.g. the effect of "Made in Germany"). A change or even a tendential nudging of an image in another direction can lead to disproportionate and incalculable consequences in the attitudes of consumers or investors. Multinational combines which find themselves directly confronted with political factors, which are frequently charged with high emotion, experience particular difficulties with their image.

The task which will increasingly face those engaged in the future development of International Marketing will be the removal from the long-term marketing decisions of companies of any randomness of development and any jungle growth of structures, in order to transplant these very decisions into the area of systematically pursued company goals and operative company policy. Companies will thus experience the necessity of Strategic International Marketing, which proceeds from clear target-setting for international business and which is integrated into the long-term planning of companies. The ultimate goal of the long-term securing of a market can be attained either by intensified and differentiated export-import efforts or by foreign investment in various forms. The choice between these alternatives is at the same time linked to the decision between an international combine strategy and a nationally oriented company strategy. At this point, therefore, clear goals must be established concerning future company policy.

F. International Strategic Marketing

1. The Strategic Planning of International Companies

The incorporation of companies into the international division of labour represents basically a long-term process through which the structure and the future development of companies will be fixed in a manner which determines their fate. The build-up of foreign business is a regularly occurring development in which companies not only have to invest know-how, time and financial resources, but which also impinges upon the self-understanding of the company concerned and must lead to the development of an internationally oriented company culture.

The expansion, the further expansion and the process of adjustment necessitated by international involvement, all profoundly influence the structure of companies: from the product range, through aspects of organisation, personnel and finance to questions of the legal form of the individual companies. Activities in the area of International Marketing, because of their structural peculiarities, require a company to adopt a strategic orientation for the totality of its decisions. International Marketing has become the essential component of the strategic planning of many German industrial companies, as it has for companies in other export-oriented countries (for example Japan or the Netherlands).

The strategic planning of the international involvement of companies is closely tied to the strategies of International Marketing. Decisions taken by companies to build up export business on important foreign markets develop in the course of events a dynamic of their own, which can be changed or completely abandoned either not at all or only by entailing difficulties which would threaten the very existence of the companies. The long-term nature and the low revisability of international involvements become particularly clear with decisions concerning the undertaking of foreign investments. Even ignoring the politico-economic difficulties encountered in a country like South Africa, the socio-political ones in a country like Iran or the inflationary problems in a country like Brazil, companies are neither able nor willing to abandon their foreign investments and involvements at short notice, even when confronted by actual difficulties of great size.

Decisions concerning International Marketing are mostly lasting ones and it is only in the long term that they can be either changed or corrected. It therefore becomes all the more important for companies to clarify their goals for themselves and then to make their own decisions commercially viable. International Marketing is therefore largely a matter of Strategic International Marketing. This strategic component of International Marketing has not previously been given adequate consideration in the literature of business management theory. Instead one finds prominence being given to operational and tactical decisions about prices and reductions, the logistics of distribution and communications policy. The central strategic significance of International Marketing for the existence of companies and the related orientation of International Marketing towards strategic decisions have not yet been sufficiently analysed.

Interviews with various companies have indicated that many German companies do not make strategic decisions in any conscious or deliberate manner whatsoever, but usually only make operational or tactical decisions in the area of International Marketing, and in the course of further development these decisions then attain a strategic significance. It can therefore be said that the strategic decision process in a large number of German firms follows the pattern **Bottom-Up**.

The tactical and the operative decisions confer a normative power on the factual. It is only in the course of further development that companies realise that their original decision was a strategic one as well, which they must then retrospectively consolidate and fulfill.

By contrast, the large U.S. combines and the Japanese world firms make strategic decisions more often in accordance with the model **Top-Down**.

In this case the operational and tactical decisions are undertaken within a pre-arranged strategic framework.

In reality, many international companies operate within a process in which the individual decision levels and the various decision horizons overlap (Diagram 10).

This allows us to categorise various types of connection between decision and effect:

1) strategic basic decision with direct effect on the action of companies,
2) operational and tactical decisions with direct effect on the actions of companies,
3) direct influence of the strategic decisions on the operational and tactical ones,
4) indirect influence of operational and tactical decisions on strategic decisions about the normative force of the factual,
5) repercussions of changes in the international competitive situation on the strategic, operational and tactical decisions.

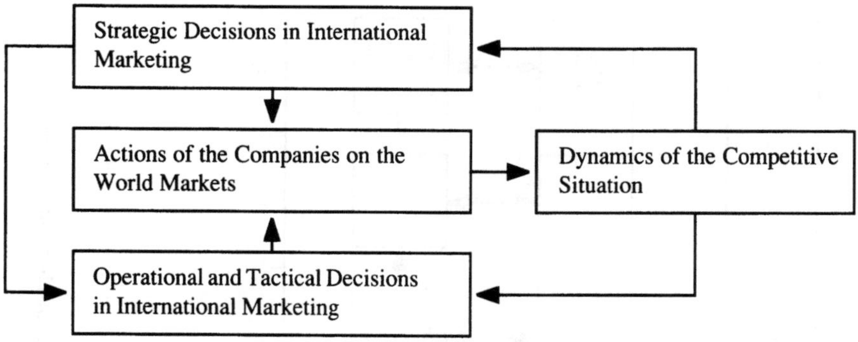

Diagram 10. The influence of strategic and operational decisions on the international activities of companies

The strategic areas of decision in International Marketing require a clearly higher level of coordination in companies. Whereas operational and tactical decisions are made at the level of company departments and executives, responsibility for the strategic decisions must be taken by the company directors.

Incorporation into the company planning system is of central importance. It often happens that strategic plans are not laid out with any great degree of formality and restrict themselves to statements of the targets set by company policy with respect to profit potential, at any rate up to the quantitative consequences. Operational plans on the other hand are formulated in a much more exact manner and represent in the case of the large companies complex works of calculation in which the financial effects and the profitability of individual operational sub-plans are set down, just as is the interweaving of these into the overall plan of the company. The tactical plans are set up at short notice and assume the character of ad hoc decisions. They influence the course of individual deals and transactions under the aspect of short-term considerations of profitability and decisions about liquidity.

Planning, decision and realisation are closely connected in the case of foreign activities. The overlapping of the levels of planning, decision, control and action in the undertaking of foreign investment is indicated by Diagram 11.

This overview makes clear the high level of coordination which becomes necessary between separate levels of management when companies become involved in foreign activities. One also notices here the great importance of **synergistic effects**, which play a central role in Strategic International Marketing. By synergistic effect is meant the additional competence in decision-making which arises out of the cooperation of different departments within a company.

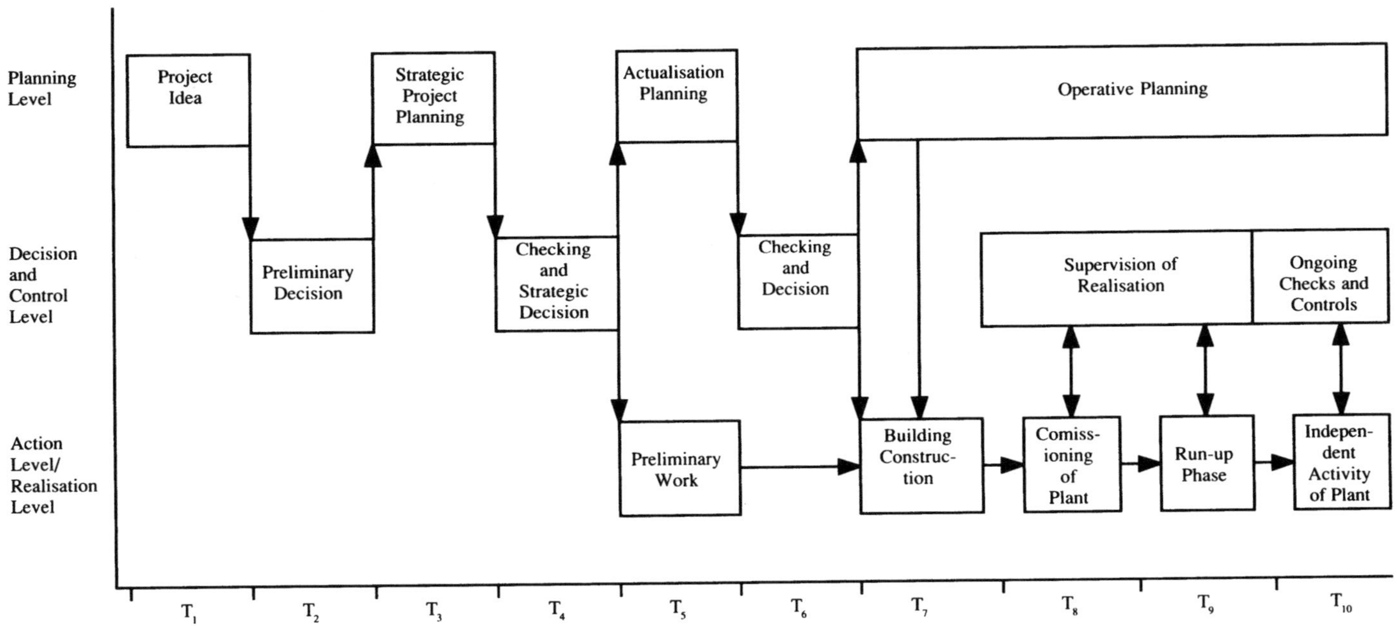

Diagram 11. The planning, decision and realisation of foreign activities[1]

[1] Diagram taken from: Arbeitskreis Karenberg/Meissner der Schmalenbach-Gesellschaft, Auslandsaktivitäten deutscher Unternehmen, Chancen der Zukunftssicherung, (BfAi) Cologne 1983, p. 34.

Strategic International Marketing is coupled to a series of conditions and preconditions. In addition to the need for internal coordination there is also a requirement for an unusually large, and above all an internationally differentiated, supply of information. Strategic International Marketing can be pursued in a responsible and rational manner only with a maximum of reliable and relevant information. In view of the overwhelming importance of information for Strategic International Marketing, this topic will be dealt with in a special section.[2]

Companies must use this information as starting-point especially for analyses of risks and countries, which will provide them with the basis for the identification and selection of possible strategies. It is noticeable that legal, taxational and financial considerations must be included to an increasing degree in the decision processes of International Marketing.

2. Long-Term Planning and the Setting of Targets in Foreign Activities

The preconditions for long-term strategic planning, which is to determine the structures of a company in a lasting fashion, are an overall company philosophy and the setting of the particular goals which are to be followed by a company.

The strategic long-term planning of foreign activity is influenced by the prevalent company philosophy and by the basic interests of separate companies, or of combinations of companies, in **"going international"**.

The decision to become involved in foreign activities can be triggered either by the process of development on a foreign market or by increasing market saturation on the home market. In this situation it still happens, now as before, that companies grow into their foreign activities without having undergone in advance any conscious preparatory planning process which takes explicit account of the significance and the length of time involved in the procedure. Other companies, and this applies especially to multinational companies, follow by contrast a company policy which has a planned international orientation.

---

[2] See Chapter G. The Informational Bases of Strategic International Marketing.

But even those companies which have simply grown into foreign business arrive at a point where they must clearly recognise that the securing of their long-term existence has in the meantime come to depend on their international orientation. They must therefore acknowledge and accept internationalisation as a predominant element in their general company planning.

This basic international orientation is now steadily increasing with a large number of medium-sized companies as well; as their export quotas and their foreign investments grow these firms direct their attention intensively and consciously towards the opportunities of the world market.[3]

A company philosophy which is formed against an international background and continues to be influenced by it requires companies to mould their decision processes and their planning to correspond to both the opportunities and the necessities of international market segments. An internationally oriented company planning will make itself felt not least in the organisation of companies and in their personnel policy, as well as in internationally oriented financial and monetary policies and in the inclusion of international opportunities for research and development. Internationalisation becomes the dominant ideal towards which the separate activities of the companies must be directed in a planned manner.

Even with large German industrial companies one still occasionally encounters a hesitant attitude towards this international basic stance. The companies still see themselves primarily as national companies, which just happen to have considerable foreign business. This fundamentally national attitude then prevents such companies from pursuing international market and development opportunities in a consistent and future-oriented manner, and from building them into their strategic company concept.

The long-term planning of the international activities of companies finds particular expression in the motives for undertaking foreign activities – and especially in the motives for undertaking direct investments abroad. Investigations of American and German companies[4] have shown that market-related factors are to the fore. Besides these, existing impediments to trade play an important role. Cost factors and medium-term expectations of profit are by comparison of only secondary importance.

The consequence for Strategic International Marketing consists in the fact that the **orientation towards the world market** must stand in the foreground of the strategic and planning process. The other motives for foreign activities have only a complementary and reinforcing function. The opportunities and

[3] Cf. Dülfer, E., Die Auswirkungen der Internationalisierung auf Führung und Organisationsstruktur mittelständischer Unternehmen, in: BFuP, 1985, No. 6, pp. 493–514.
[4] Cf. Jahrreiß, W., Zur Theorie der Direktinvestinvestitionen im Ausland, Berlin 1984, pp. 278–295.

risks of foreign activities therefore cannot be judged solely and sufficiently in the light of their short- and medium-term effects, as this only becomes possible in long-term perspective. The quantitative judgment of the individual activities is not made any easier by this. Long-term international decisions are burdened by a high measure of uncertainty, both because of the temporal horizon of such decisions and because of the great number and variety of influencing factors in international markets and market segments. Strategic International Marketing must therefore concern itself above all with creating the informational preconditions for the planning decisions and with developing and utilising special and appropriate methods for the strategic decisions.

The international planning of companies differs in its content and partly also in its methodology from national planning. Traditional business management theory still often allows itself to be guided by the idea that its system and its theoretical concepts are of such general import that a distinction between national and international management is superfluous and artificial. Nevertheless the reality of company leadership indicates that fundamental distinctions have to made here, and that it is precisely the internationally successful companies which bring an appropriate and differentiated attitude to their international business and utilise the corresponding information and planning techniques, as well as specific strategic instruments.[5] It is obvious that German business management theory has much ground to make up in this area, in research as well as in teaching.

The differences between national and international planning can be characterised as follows:[6]

National Planning	International Planning
1) Only one language and nationality.	1) Several languages/ several nationalities/ various sociocultural factors of influence.
2) Relatively homogeneous markets.	2) Fragmented and varied markets.
3) Availability of data, normally exact and simple obtaining of data	3) Obtaining of data very difficult, usually involves significantly higher cost and commitment of personnel.

[5] These two areas will be discussed in following Chapters G and H.

[6] Presentation follows Phatak, A. V., Managing Multinational Corporations, New York, Washington, London 1974, p. 149, cited in: Welge, M., Management in deutschen multinationalen Unternehmungen, Stuttgart 1980, p. 212.

National Planning	International Planning
4) Political factors of influence are relatively unimportant.	4) Political factors of influence are numerous and of vital importance.
5) Relative independence from government influence.	5) Integration into national economic planning; governments influence company decisions.
6) The individual company has a relatively small influence on the environment.	6) Serious disruption caused by large companies.
7) Chauvinism is helpful.	7) Chauvinism is a hindrance.
8) Relatively stable environmental situation.	8) Numerous environmental situations, of which many are very unstable (but many promise high returns).
9) Homogeneous financial climate.	9) Various types of financial climate, which range from over-conservative to very inflationary.
10) A single currency.	10) Various currencies with different levels of stability and buying power.
11) "Rules of the game" clear and understood.	11) "Rules of the game" are varied, subject to change and unclear.
12) The management is used to assuming responsibility and employing financial control methods.	12) The management is usually autonomous and not familiar with budgets and other instruments of control.

3. Risk and Country Analysis

Strategic International Marketing is always very closely linked, in the area of trade as well as in that of investment and services, to decisions of company location in the sense of the selection of a market. In the analysis of the underlying motives for foreign involvements and market choice decisions, growth strategies can be differentiated from rationalisation strategies: growth as well as nationalisation strategies relate both to export activities and to the undertaking of foreign investments, and also have a role to play in conjunction with other possible foreign activities.[7]

Growth Strategies.

- Strategies of partial diversification,
- strategies of special intensification,
- strategies of the expansion of existing sites of production and services ("on-site expansion").

Rationalisation Strategies.

- Purification strategy
- Concentration strategy
- Strategy of partial closure of existing production sites ("on-site-contraction").

The estimation of the typical foreign trade risks and the risk analysis of countries have a central significance for the Strategic International Marketing decisions of companies. Risk estimation and country analysis are the preconditions for a market entry decision and simultaneously for the selection of an appropriate strategy (Diagram 12).

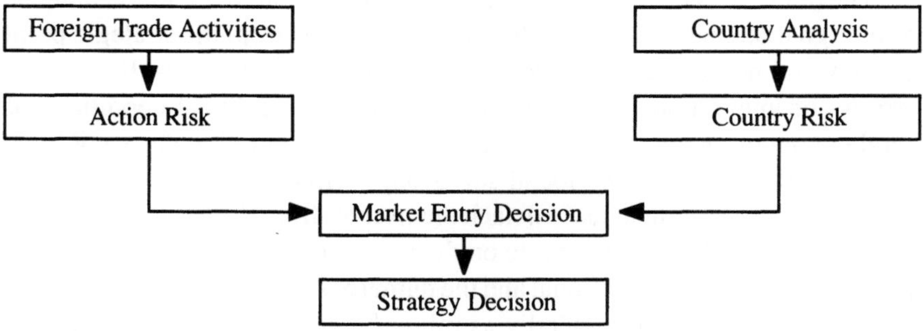

Diagram 12. Risk analysis and strategic international decisions

[7] Cf. Lüder, K., Strategische Standortplanung transnationaler industrieller Großunternehmen, in: Lück, W., Trommsdorff, V. (Eds.), Internationisierung der Unternehmung, Berlin 1982, p. 424.

The special aspects of foreign trade dealings are a consequence primarily of the nature and the intensity of the risks connected to the foreign activities. The structure, i.e. the nature and the extent of the risks, is different for every foreign activity and must be carefully studied by companies precisely from the strategic point of view.

The risk of foreign activities is related to the **commercial risks**, therefore to such risks as those of transport and storage, assemblage and postponement, as well as to those which arise in the context of guarantees.[8] In addition to this political risks play a fundamental role in International Marketing.

The **country risk** arises especially from the economic, social and political development of a country, which finds expression in the structures of the economic and trade policies, the conversion and transfer conditions, and the course of the rate of exchange. From the strategic point of view, the substitution risk plays a significant role. **A substitution risk** emerges precisely when previous export supplies have been particularly successful. In such situations the governments of many developing , threshold and state trade countries follow an economic and trade policy aimed at replacing previous imports by local production. So as not to have to abandon such markets entirely, the previous exporters find themselves forced into undertaking foreign investments in the countries concerned – often in the legally prescribed form of joint ventures with minority participation. Foreign investments thus frequently become instruments of long-term company policy for the securing and the further expansion of international markets and market segments, which were previously opened up by exports, and from which traditional markets companies do not now wish to be driven.

The **political risk** cannot be discussed purely as a matter for the techniques of foreign trade, but must be analysed by companies from the strategic point of view and neutralised as far as possible. Political risk arises through the process of integration into the existing cultural and political conditions of another country and in spite of efforts to preserve neutrality, so as not to be classified as alien by other social sub-groups within the host country. The tendency of many companies to detach themselves from the political development of the world and concentrate on the economic opportunities cannot, in view of the existing international and the numerous internal political tensions, be maintained as single-mindedly as might be desirable from the strategic point of view. Internationally active companies must therefore reckon in every case with a certain amount of political risk and adjust themselves to it in the long run. Examples of countries with high political risk may be found among those states which are involved in military conflict (such as until recently Iran

---

[8] Cf. Zimmermann, A., Spezifische Risiken des Auslandsgeschäfts, in: Dichtl, E., Issing, O. (Eds.), Exporte als Herausforderung für die deutsche Wirtschaft, Cologne 1984, pp. 105–139.

and Iraq), which lie in areas of political tension (such as Israel and the Lebanon), in which there is direct political upheaval (such as in Nicaragua or Afghanistan) or in which there is a marked process of internal political destabilisation (such as in the Philippines in 1985 or at the beginning of the 80's in the People's Republic of Poland).

A further possible option for companies lies in fully accepting the political risk and becoming themselves motors of political development. But even the great multinational combines or the powerful Japanese trading-houses are no longer, under the present conditions of the world economy and world politics, in any position decisively to shape political developments in other parts of the world to their will. Every attempt in this direction implies an extremely high political risk, which is not rationally calculable either for the companies of for their leading executives.

The political risk of a country and the risk of economic development are evaluated with the aid of indicators. In principle, what is involved here are descriptive elements which are intended to predict future developments with a certain degree of probability. The suitability of certain factors or descriptive elements as indicators reminds one of experiences which were made with prophecy in earlier periods. Finally there are also conventions which have been formed in the course of using indicators, and which then enter into the prognosis.

The use of indicators requires in each case an integration of subjective opinions and impressions with quantitative methods of the recording of past values. No indicator can remove the basic uncertainty of future developments. Nevertheless it forces management to ponder carefully its future-oriented strategies, since the significance and the effect of these indicators must be looked at closely.

Indicators for assessing country risks are composed of the indicators of economic development and of political risks:[9]

A. Economic Indicators.

1) Gross National Product (GNP),
2) growth in GNP in previous years,
3) income per head,
4) price development,
5) employment and rate of unemployment,
6) foreign trade,
7) balance of payments
8) currency reserves and extent of international debt.

---

[9] Cf. Leontiades, J., Multinational Corporate Strategy, Lexington/Mass., Toronto 1985, p. 161.

B. Political and Social Indicators.

1) Political environment,
   form of government,
   historical development,
   party spectrum,
   basic programme of the parties,
   analysis of voters.
   role and influence of the military,
   attitude towards foreign firms,
   role and influence of state on business,
   religious and ethnic differences;

2) Internal political stability;

3) Foreign political alliances and tensions
   – membership of political blocks,
   – military conflicts,
   – diplomatic tensions,
   – trade-political conflicts.

The evaluation of the risks associated with individual countries requires both reliable information and a standard of judgement and measurement. Such standards arise out of the international experience of companies, or else they are based on external know-how, for example that of business consultants, bank representatives or state institutions, which can draw upon the necessary experience, such as for example the commercial departments of the diplomatic consulates or the interstate Chambers of Commerce abroad.
On the basis of an assessment of the action risk and of the country risk a risk profile can then be constructed for individual planned foreign activities (Cf. Table 14).

Strategic International Marketing must assume the task of deciding with the aid of such country risk profiles, upon matters of market entry, market involvement and if need be, market exit. In this context companies must see to it that they select those very markets which open up the greatest opportunities for the future.[10]

In a further step the appropriate strategies for the markets selected must then be found, and these decisions in turn must be differentiated according to individual products and product groups, markets and market segments, as well

[10] Cf. Meffert, H., Althans, J., Internationales Marketing, Stuttgart 1982, pp. 71 ff.

as according to the nature of the involvement. From this results a three-dimensional field of decision, in which the individual strongpoints of the foreign involvements of the companies can be localised.[11]

Table 14. Risk profile of foreign activities

Type of Risk	Intensity of the Risk Expected	I	II	III	IV	V
A) Action Risk						
1. Economic Risk						
2. Exchange and Transfer Risk						
3. Transport and Storage Risk						
4. Contractual Risks (Guarantees)						
5. Substitution Risk						
B) Country Risk						
1. Development Risk						
2. Debt Risk						
3. Risk from the Political Environment						
4. Internal Political Risk						
5. External Political Risks						

I – very high risk II – high risk III – normal risk IV – slight risk V – no risk

4. Identification and Selection of Strategy: Unitary or Differentiated International Marketing

When they decide upon involvement in certain countries companies find themselves face to face with a core problem of Strategic International Marketing, and that is the question as to whether the international markets and market segments are to be opened up and treated with a world-wide unitary strategy of **standardisation** or whether in each case nationally and even regionally adjusted strategies of **differentiation** are to be employed.

The American multinational combines have to a very large extent followed the model of a world-wide unitary marketing concept,[12] whereas the European

[11] See on this point also Diagram 30, Chapter H. 612 Cf. Keegan, W. J., Multinational Marketing Management, Englewood Cliffs/N.J. 1974, pp. 235 ff.

[12] Cf. Keegan, W. J., Multinational Marketing Management, Englewood Cliffs/N.J. 1974, pp. 235 ff

companies, and this applies to German companies in particular, tended rather to follow an internationally differentiated strategy. The developments of recent years indicate, however, that large American and Japanese combines are now tending to adapt themselves in a more pronounced and a more precise manner to the national markets and to regional particularities in the individual areas and regions of the world, whereas German companies are emphasising their international identities more strongly, for example by creating an internationally unitary company image, or by offering the customer internationally standardised branded articles or service packages.

A mixture of standardised and differentiated strategic elements is nowadays normal. Companies strive, for example, to aim some parts of their sales packages as accurately as possible at the national markets, e.g. the final technical design or the financial conditions, whereas other parts, perhaps in the area of communications or of fundamental decisions on product policy, are given an internationally unitary configuration insofar as possible.

The dilemma of decision between standardised and differentiated international marketing strategies arises not just in the case of exports, but also and especially with foreign investments. The growing nationalism of many countries and their increasing international self-awareness now make it very difficult to avoid adjusting to the national attitudes, conditions and regulations of these countries, and this extends to filling the top positions with local citizens and to engaging advertising agencies from the country of investment. In the case of advertising it is above all the national subsidiaries of the international advertising agencies which are drawing an increasing proportion of the internationally oriented business to them; they thereby promote a new tendency towards the synchronisation of the market-specific orientation and the international standardisation of marketing, and to this extent they frequently decide the issue between differentiated and standardised strategies by the making of compromises.

The strategic concept of International Marketing demands of companies a high level of sensitization towards both national and regional differences. A standardisation takes place at the head of the combine, which takes on the task of a holding company, including the orientation towards an image which is internationally synchronised and made as unitary as possible throughout the world. The success of internationally unitary marketing pursued by some individual world companies (for example Coca Cola, IBM or hotel chains) can only be transferred to other products or other producers to a limited extent. The individual constituent companies or combines follow strategies which are more strongly differentiated along national lines, in order to be able to adjust to national or regional market conditions as they occur.

The decision between a standardised or differentiated strategy for working a market must be made specifically in each case. The prevailing company philosophy is of great importance here, as is the company culture which has been developed in conjuction with an internationally oriented company strategy.

5. The Strategic Concept of International Marketing

The development of a stategic concept for International Marketing proceeds by way of various steps and stages. To the formulation of global company goals is added the process of the procurement of information which, against a background of country profiles, undertakes an analysis of strengths and weaknesses for the company concerned or for a branch of industry. To this in turn are added the formulation of an orientation system and in a further step the determination of the basic strategies. This is then followed by the planning of marketing concepts for the individual national markets (Diagrams 13 and 14).

The results from the individual international sub-markets, as well as changes in the configuration of strengths and weaknesses, e.g. as a result of increased international competition, or new developments in the country risk, must then lead to processes of adjustment in the basic strategies or in the general system of orientation, and even in certain cases to changes in the company goals. The aspect of flexibility is of particular significance for Strategic International Marketing.

Diagram 13. The stages in the conception of strategies in International Marketing

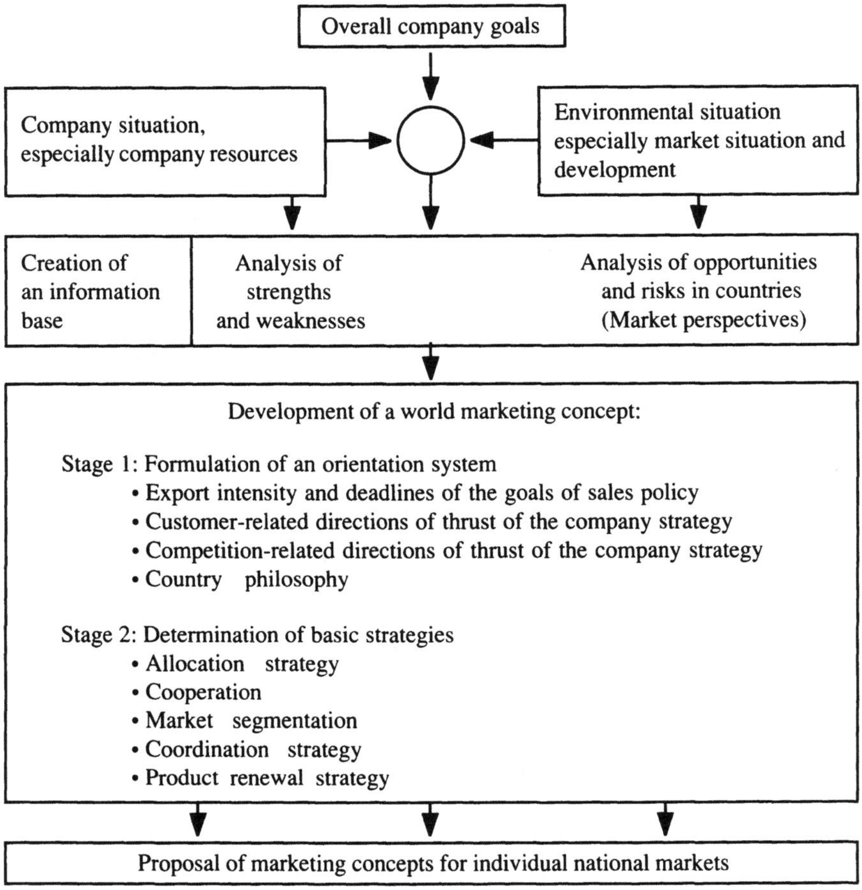

Diagram 14. Development of a conception of International Marketing [13]

[13] Diagram taken from Raffée, H., Segler, K., Marketingstrategien im Export, in: Dichtl, E., Issing, O. (Eds.), Exporte als Herausforderung für die deutsche Wirtschaft, Cologne 1984, p. 280.

G. The Informational Bases of Strategic International Marketing

1. The Significance of Information in Strategic International Marketing

Strategic decisions make it necessary for companies to develop a specific information culture. Within the framework of this information culture it is important for companies to develop a system for obtaining and processing those items of information which are of significance for the structural decisions.

An information culture means that in order to obtain the bases necessary for making decisions companies cannot depend, or cannot depend exclusively, upon previous experience and cannot be satisfied with arbitrary ad hoc information, such as might come from personal conversation, foreign visits or the reports of representatives, but that they consciously and systematically comprehend and evaluate the variety of information relevant to decisions. For this reason companies must build up and utilise an appropriate information system, which is oriented very precisely towards the informational requirements of this company in the context of its strategic decisions.

In the area of marketing an absolute essential for every company is the availability of an information system which can be used as the basis for marketing decisions. Traditionally foreign trade marketing is bound up with careful and comprehensive information work.[1] Within the framework of the strategic decisions and planning of companies for foreign trade, informational requirements acquire a particular significance.

Information for Strategic International Marketing must be used in the first instance for the **recognition of patterns**. It is therefore not just a matter of collecting individual pieces of information from the areas of business, technology or politics, but of so utilising synergistic effects while linking these pieces of information with each other and evaluating them, that it becomes possible to forecast the basic patterns of future development with a sufficient degree of

[1] Cf. Ringel, K, Exportmarktforschung als Informationsaufgabe, Cologne and Opladen 1963; Stahr, G, Auslandsmarketing , Vol. 1, Marktanalyse, Stuttgart 1979, pp. 32 ff.

clarity and reliability. These analyses and the prognoses constructed on them should serve to identify future opportunities, draw attention to possible sources of danger and pose strategic key questions on which the strategic success and therefore the existence of the firm will depend in the long term.[2]

2. Methodological Aspects of the Obtaining of Information

a) Sources of Information

The high demands which are made with regard to the completeness and accuracy of the information which is to be used as the basis for strategic decisions in International Marketing are paralleled by the requirement of a correspondingly careful and differentiated methodological procedure. Even medium-sized companies can carry out sufficiently thorough foreign market research at a relatively favourable cost by checking and comparing the reports of foreign subsidiaries or representative offices and the information gained on business journeys with the available secondary information.

It is precisely this combination of secondary information with the collection of personal impressions on business journeys which represents one of the most frequently used data bases for decisions on the selection of markets. In the markets selected the data basis is complemented by systematic primary research. The information then available serves as a basis for strategic decisions (Diagram 15), e.g. whether a market should be opened up by intensifying export business or by undertaking foreign investment in the form of a joint venture, or whether and to what extent the successful working of a market requires a specifically differentiated performance or communications strategy.

The importance of the content and the expenditure on the individual stages of information-gathering is determined by the various market conditions. In traditional markets, on which a company is very well established, the information which is important for the future can be obtained by personal communication, whereas in those countries which are to be examined for market entry, it is mainly secondary sources which are drawn upon as preparation for a decision concerning market entry. But with especially far-reaching strategic decisions a first-hand survey is unavoidable when reliable information is required about the demand, the competition and the further development of the market.

[2] Cf. Aaker, D. A., Strategic Market Management, New York, 1984, pp. 92 ff.

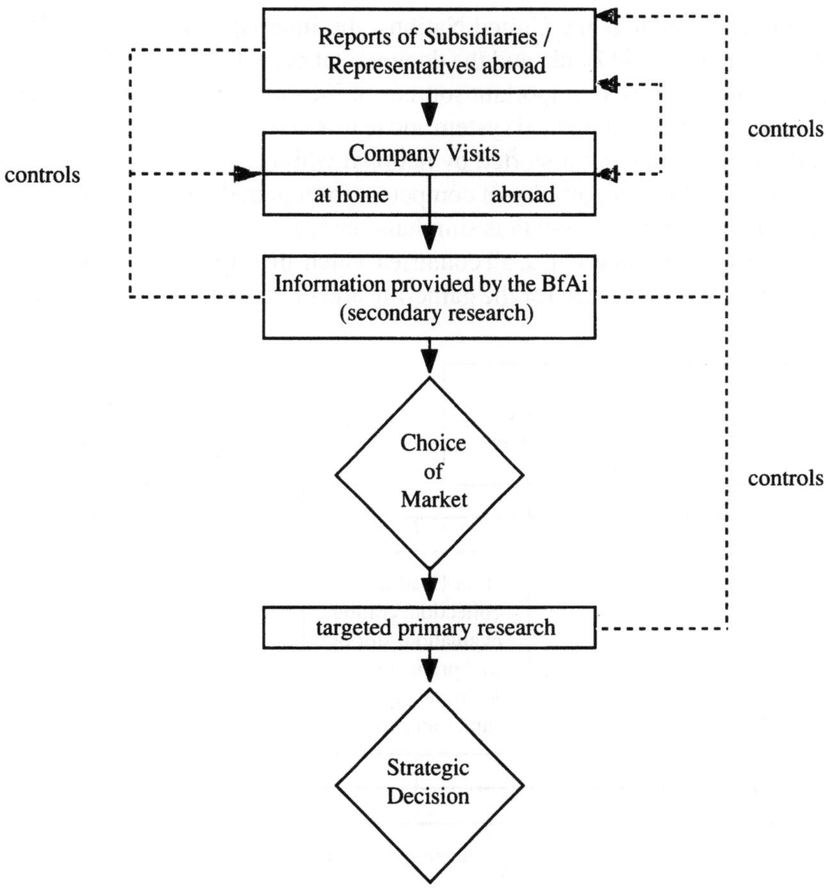

Diagram 15. Information and decision system for foreign activities[3]

b) Secondary Research

For foreign market research in general and Strategic International Marketing in particular secondary research represents the essential informational prerequisite if one wishes to be in a position to judge and estimate the future markets and the opportunities and risks of individual strategies.

For secondary research companies have a large number of possible sources of information available to them.[4] The reports and statistics of international

[3] Taken from Meissner, H.G., So erobern Sie schwierige Märkte, in: Rationalisierungs-Kuratorium der Deutschen Wirtschaft (Ed.), Export-Konferenz 1984, Düsseldorf 1984, p. 29.
[4] Cf. Berekoven, L., Internationales Marketing, 2nd Edn., Herne and Berlin 1985, p. 67.

organisations such as the United Nations, the International Monetary Fund (IMF) and the World Bank, and the documentation of GATT, the OECD and the EC today represent important sources of information, because they have developed a unitary statistical system and to this extent make comparable data available which are not distorted by national whims.

Because of the importance of competent foreign trade information for the decisions of companies and thus simultaneously for the position in the world economy of individual states, all countries which are important in world trade have set up a state bureau for the gathering and dissemination of information

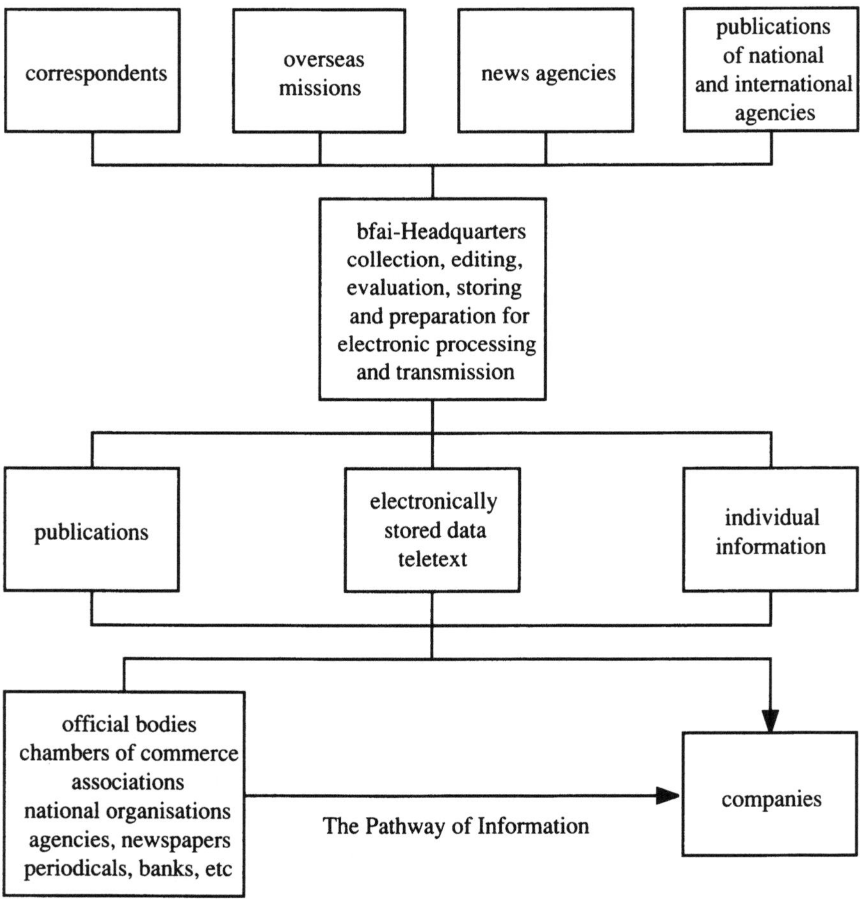

Diagram 16. The BfAI as a data pool for foreign trade information[5]

[5] Taken from n.a.; Informationen über die Märkte der Welt, in: Ernährungswirtschaft, No. 9, 1985, p. 33.

on foreign trade. In West Germany this task falls to the lot of the **Bundesstelle für Aussenhandelsinformation** (BfAI) (Federal Office for Foreign Trade Information) in Cologne, which is a subordinate department of the Federal Ministry of Trade.

The BFAI has the task of obtaining foreign trade information, processing it and passing it on to companies. The information system of the BfAI is shown by Diagram 16.

Strategic International Marketing is substantially based upon prognoses of future development in individual countries and sub-markets and in the world economy as a whole. Thus it is also always essential for the secondary material to be capable of aiding the task of prognosis.

As a safeguard for strategic decisions cooperation with academic institutes is advisable, as these have a greater overview of individual developments and at the same time have available to them the methodological prerequisites for strategic prognosis.

c) Primary Research

Primary research is employed for the decision of strategy in selected markets as well as for decisions about the composition of the individual components of the marketing mix, such as e.g. the content of advertising, price differentiation or distribution channels. In the context of Strategic International Marketing primary research has mostly a complementary function: thus decisions on market entry and the corresponding choice of strategy are still made now as before in the first instances on the basis of secondary analyses, whereas primary research comes into its own in the selection of market processing strategies and particularly with operational and tactical decisions.

International trade fairs play an important part in the obtaining of information in connection with Strategic International Marketing. It is true that the primary informational function of fairs is for current business and thereby for tactical and operational decisions, but they are useful as well as instruments for obtaining information for strategic decisions in International Marketing. It thus happens that on the occasion of many international fairs additional symposia are organised at which reports are presented on new developments and trends and new research results are presented. To this extent it is precisely at trade fairs that technical information can be obtained at a major level. Furthermore, subject-related communication and personal conversations at trade fairs also transmit commercial, political and social information, and they give particulars on cultural background, so that if all this is systematically evaluated important information for Strategic International Marketing can be obtained.

3. Areas of Information

a) Customer Behaviour

The peculiarity of international market research consists in the fact that aspects of the behaviour or the attitudes of consumers and investors which are self-evident to companies selling on the home market must now be clarified by market research. This gives rise to the necessity of having at one's disposal a comprehensive methodological range of instruments with powerful assertive criteria.

The specific culture in which a person happens to grow up and live is decisive in the formation of attitudes and the shaping of consumer behaviour patterns. To this extent any marketing research which interests itself in international matters faces the task of examining the anthropological bases for the foreign activities of firms.[6] Essentially this is a task for secondary research, but at any rate such fundamental questions are now being increasingly drawn into the framework of investigations of attitudes and of ethnological studies in primary research.

The anthropological bases of International Marketing relate primarily to social processes, e.g. the framework of political systems and cultural conditions on the various foreign markets. Culture is understood as

"....the total way of life of a people, the social legacy which an individual receives from his group. Culture can therefore be understood as that part of the environment which has been created by man."[7]

These cultural factors play a significant role in prognosis for Strategic International Marketing. Thus the Japanese distribution systems rests on certain cultural traditions, and it is therefore very difficult for a foreign firm to achieve a sufficient share of the market in Japan. Japan is a typical market in which there exists by any standard demand and buying power for western products, and in which the trade-political preconditions for opening up the market are also met. Yet the distribution system which has been handed down either prevents marketing successes from being realised at all in Japan, or else permits progress at only a very slow rate.

The importance possessed by international consumer research both for the decisions of internationally active companies and for marketing theory has not previously been awarded sufficient attention, although there are signs that this

---

[6] Cf. Meissner, H.G., Anthropologische Grundlagen der Exportmarktforschung, Berlin 1959.
[7] Kluckhohn, C., Spiegel der Menschheit, Zürich 1951, p. 31.

situation is now changing.[8] Thus for example a model has been constructed by lifestyle 'research which links the cultural aspects of the behaviour of consumers and investors with other important criteria for the explanation and prognosis of this behaviour and in particular makes them amenable to a measure of quantification which is desirable for various decision processes.[9]

b) Analyses of Countries

Country analyses have in the meantime become a self-evident component of Strategic International Marketing. They provide extensive information on factual matters and general environmental situations which confront any company active in the country concerned, and in doing so they concentrate on the comprehension of current commercial and political economic development. Country analysis represent an important basis for the strategic decisions of internationally active companies. However a prerequisite for this is that the reports on countries which are produced by the various institutions are also systematically evaluated and used as a basis for market- and company-specific analyses and prognoses.

Country analyses are carried out both by institutions and by individual authors, e.g. by specifically interested scholars. Provincial associations produce reports about the provinces which they represent. Furthermore, carefully researched country reports are published by banks, associations of industry and the BfAI. Finally, numerous supranational and international organisations such as the OECD publish country reports.

The various groups of countries play an important part in the world economy, e.g. the threshold countries in Southeast Asia, the oil-exporting states or the group of state trade countries. Just as in the industrial countries, there is taking shape in these countries too an increasing interest in further world economic interlinking. These countries exercise quite specific influence on the dynamics of world trade, which must absolutely be taken into account in the strategic concepts of companies.

---

[8] See for example the summary in: Holzmüller, H. H., Grenzüberschreitende Konsumentenforschung, in: Marketing, Vol. 8, No. 1 (Feb 1986), pp. 45–54, or the contributions in: Tiong Tan, Chin, Sheth, Jagdish N. (Eds.), Historical Perspective in Consumer Research: National and International Perspectives, Proceedings of the Association for Consumer Research International Meeting in Singapore, July 18–20, 1985.

[9] Cf. on this point the discussion and further references to the literature in: Banning, T., Lebensstilorientierte Marketing-Theorie, Heidelberg 1987.

c) Reports on Branches of Industry

In addition to analyses of countries, international reports on branches of industry are important as an information base for strategic decisions. Here it is once more a question of presenting the differentiated development of the branches of industry in the individual sub-markets of the world and also of taking account of the expectations of the branches in the various countries. As a methodological example one may cite the analysis of the car market in the important producing countries of the world in the years 1983/1984 (Tables 15 and 16).

Reports on branches of industry are produced especially by the appropriate trade and manufacturers' associations. In addition to these however publications on specific branches of industry are also issued by banks and international organisations.

Reports on branches of industry should also always serve to make evident any relative or absolute changes in the international competitive position of companies. The development of branches of industry is thus closely connected with changes in the competitive positions of individual companies in the world economy.

d) Information on Competition

The future market opportunities and the forms of opening up and securing markets for international companies are in a special way dependent on the conditions of international competition. In the days of "classical" foreign trade competition was influenced especially by customs duties and contingencies. After the worldwide dismantling of these traditional impediments to trade, particularly by the tariff discussions of GATT and the policy integration within the European Economic Community, non-tariff barriers to trade emerged in their place, and in some cases the effect of these has contributed more to the disruption of the international structure of competition than customs tariffs and contingencies could ever have done.[10] Information for policy on competition must therefore be attained not just about competing firms, but also about, for example, the regulations and conditions governing foreign investments, or about aspects of international taxation, as these all represent important decision parameters for Strategic International Marketing.

[10] Cf. Börgers, K.-H., Quambusch, L., Export und Auslandsinvestitionen, Cologne 1985, p. 26.

Table 15. Expected developments in the car market[11]

	Produktion	New Admissions	Exports
Japan	+ 2 to + 3	+ 3 to + 5	+ 2 to + 4
USA	+15 to +20	+14 to +18	+10 to +15
West Germany	- 1 to - 4	0 to - 2	- 3 to - 5
France	- 6 to -10	- 9 to -12	- 3 to - 5
Italy	+ 5 to + 7	+ 5 to + 8	0 to - 3
Spain	+ 3 to + 6	+ 2 to + 4	+12 to +16
Great Britain	0 to + 1	0 to + 2	0
Canada	+12 to +16	+10 to +15	+15 to +20
Brazil	-15 to -20	+10 to +15	+15 to +20

The figures given are the quantitative changes expected in 1983 for 1984 in per cent to the previous year.

Table 16. Market prognoses in the car market[12]
Production, new registrations and exports in chosen countries

	Production		New Registrations		Exports	
	1983[1]	1984[2]	1983[1]	1984[2]	1983[1]	1984[2]
Japan	7.152	+1.3	3.136	+7.0	3.806	+2.0
USA	6.781	+28.7	8.924	+26.6	538	+24.5[4]
West Germany	3.878	-13.1	2.427	-3.1	2.189	-9.7
France	2.961	-10.6	2.018	+15.0	1.614	-3.7
Italy	1.396	+13.4	1.512	+4.1[3]	492	-2.6
Spain	1.142	+1.1[3]	550	-3.6	613	+28.3[4]
Great Britain	1.045	-8.4	1.792	+2.4	274	-0.3[4]
Brazil	774	-17.6	.	.	138	-
Canada	969	+11.0	830	+16.3[3]	867	+47.3[5]
Australia	317	.	434	.	.	.
Sweden	345	+9.5[5]	217	+12.9[4]	208	.
Belgium	262	.	357	.	252	.
Mexico	207	.	192	.	.	.
World production	29.846	.	.	.	.	.

1 Figures represent thousands of units.
2 calculations based on the development of the first half year of 1984.
3 Calculations based on the development from January to May 1984.
4 Calculations based on the development from January to April 1984.
5 Calculations based on the development from January to March 1984.

[11] Taken from: Commerzbank, (Eds.), Business Notes of Sep./Oct. 1984.
[12] Taken from: Commerzbank, (Eds.), Business Notes of Sep./Oct. 1984.

Table 17. Matrix of international competition[13]

Intensity of Competition \ Transfer Conditions	Favourable	Unfavourable
High	strong international price competition e.g. USA	Full exploitation of the market potential not possible e.g. People's Republic of China
low	Relatively little international competition, effort spent on opening up the market becomes the decisive criterion, e.g. Japan	Limited possibilities for international competition e.g. People's Republic of Poland

The future world trade system is of central importance here. For the international decisions of companies it is essential that the liberal world trade system, which was built up in the years following the end of the Second World War, continues to function. A functioning world trade system requires the great world trading partners, especially the EC, the USA and Japan to play an active vanguard role. Every dramatic change in the world trade system, such as the pushing-through of a "just" world economic order as many developing countries see this, represents for companies an external risk which is still scarcely calculable and which would have consequences for all strategic international decisions. There is therefore a wide measure of common ground between world economic efforts to uphold a free world trade system and the interests of companies. The existing liberal system of the world economy is therefore the prerequisite for the companies' being able to pursue Strategic International Marketing.

The conditions of competition on international markets are influenced both by the existing regulations of trade and currency policies and by the extent of effective international competition on individual markets.

[13] Taken from: Meissner, H.G., So erobern Sie schwierige Märkte, in: Rationalisierungs-Kuratorium der Deutschen Wirtschaft (Eds.), Export Conference 1984, Düsseldorf 1984, p. 32.

The possibilities of action open to companies may thus be expressed in the form of a competition matrix (Table 17), which simultaneously makes clear the formational possibilities (in the sense of portfolio strategies) which are available to International Marketing.

It is therefore a precondition for Strategic International Marketing to obtain in good time reliable information about the regulations on competitive policy in the individual countries and in the major world trading groups, so as to be in a position to make an analysis of the transfer conditions, both those now existing and those to be expected, against a background of the market potential to be expected. Such information on conditions of competition comes in particular from both state and supranational sources, whereas the direct market information comes primarily from commercial sources. The task facing companies is to check these two areas of information against each other and to combine them. Strategic International Marketing is characterised precisely by the synergistic effects arising from such combinations across quite different areas. The future of the world economy will depend not just on companies, but neither will it depend solely on governments or on international organisations, but it will depend in a very pronounced manner on the cooperation of state, supranational and company activities.
This requires of companies the construction and the utilisation of an information system, which is directed simultaneously towards both market-related developments and those affecting competition policy. In concrete terms, this means that the tasks of information in the field of business management have to be integrated with those in the field of world commerce. But since it happens only in exceptional cases that management information and information on world commerce are found together among the same people and in the same departments, companies must see to it that an appropriate coordination takes place.

e) Information on Technology

Important indicators of the development and transfer processes in the world economy are the varying technological levels or one might say the varying levels of technological availability of products, processes and services. The availability of technology, and particularly of high technology, represents the decisive factor in the international competitiveness of individual companies and countries.[14]

[14] Cf. BMWi (Eds.), Hochtechnologien und internationale Wettbewerbsfähigkeit der deutschen Wirtschaft, Document No. 263 July 1984.

Assessment of the competitive situation in individual markets (country analysis) and of the factors influencing competition must therefore take place against a background of, and in conjuction with, appropriate technological information. The following are taken to be goods of a high technological order:

> Aeroplanes, office machinery and automated data processing, electrical machines and apparatus (including signals technology, switching circuits), communications technology, measurement and control technology, optical, medical, and photographic apparatus, medical and pharmaceutical products (medicaments), plastics and synthetic fibres, motors and powered machines (turbines), chemical fertilisers and pesticides, inorganic chemicals, reception and reproductive apparatus for picture and sound (including TV, radio).

The basic dynamics of the world economy are in the meantime being acted out in these areas of high technology. The international market shares in the high technologies have evolved as follows in recent years (Table 18):

Table 18. Export shares in high technology goods[15]

	1972	1976	1980	1982
USA	32.2	34.1	35.3	40.2
Japan	13.0	18.2	18.2	20.3
Germany	26.3	21.7	20.0	17.0

In assessing these statistics, there arise problems of the delimitation of technologies. Nevertheless the trend is clear that market shares in high technology are rearranging to the disadvantage of West German firms. At the same time it must be kept in mind that the share of high technologies in world trade is increasing. In the context of foreign investments, technology transfer plays a key role, so that altogether the influence of technology, and of high technology in particular, on the further development of world trade and of the world economy is extremely large.

Plant construction is of central importance for the participation of West German companies in the international division of labour and in world economic development. Under this heading come the construction and starting-up of complex plants, for example smelting-works, rolling-mills, power stations, industrial plants for the building and building materials industry, organic chemistry and electrotechnology. In 1984 the export share for German plant construction amounted to over 60% of the total orders received.[16] The

[15] Data taken from: Deutsche Bundesbank, Company Report, 1983, p. 59.

[16] Cf. Arbeitsgemeinschaft Großanlagenbau in: VDMA, (Eds.), Position Report 1984, Frankfurt/M. 1985, p. 9.

important buying countries here are the developing countries, the OPEC countries and the state trade countries. The largest customers are listed in Table 19.

Table 19. Orders received in the plant construction sector according to country in millions of DM[17]

	1985	1984	1983
People's Republic of China	2356	473	118
USA	749	801	329
Libya	536	404	260
USSR	485	627	539
Iran	457	198	234
Turkey	416	478	249
Indonesia	388	130	360
India	339	113	417
Australia	337	32	119
Saudi Arabia	304	972	287

For their Strategic International Marketing companies therefore require a **technology information system** in addition to the traditional information on countries and branches of industry; it is also required to complement the information necessary to their competitive policies. Such systems can be set up today with the aid of international technology data banks. They provide essential information both for export business and for undertaking foreign investments, as well as for the acquisition or sale of licences.

[17] Data taken from Arbeitsgemeinschaft Großanlagenbau in: VDMA, (Eds.), Position Report 1985, Frankfurt/M.1986, p. 37.

H. Methods of Strategic International Marketing

1. The Structuring of Strategic International Marketing Decisions

Decisions and planning processes in Strategic International Marketing are subject to a substantially increased measure of uncertainty.[1] This uncertainty may be traced principally to discontinuities in the world market. It is therefore always necessary to consider Strategic International Marketing under the additional aspect of the management of discontinuities.[2]

When structuring strategic marketing decisions in foreign trade, the analysis of three different areas is of preeminent importance:

1) How will the international division of labour develop and change in the planning period? What "erratic" events will influence world trade?
2) How will the international position of the company concerned change, in what state is its international strength and weakness profile?
3) In what way and with what method can the position which the company seeks in the world economy be secured and expanded – in view of the expected development of the international division of labour with its typical discontinuities?

To answer these questions it is necessary to integrate the international activities of companies into their general management strategy. International strategies, including the strategies of International Marketing, must not be seen in isolation from the company as a whole, but must be discussed along the lines of the strategic basic concept (Table 20) which may be traced back to Ansoff.[3]

---

[1] Cf. Albach, H., Strategische Unternehmensplanung bei erhöhter Unsicherheit, in: ZfB, Vol. 48, No.8, pp. 702–715.
[2] See on this point the contributions in Macharzina, K. (Ed.), Diskontinuitätenmanagement, Berlin 1984.
[3] Cf. Ansoff, I., Management-Strategie, Munich 1966, p.135.

Table 20. Matrix of growth strategies

Products \ Markets	existing	new
existing	market penetration and exploitation	market creation
new	expansion of product policy	diversification

Strategic International Marketing is primarily brought into play in connection with the opening-up of new international markets (by market creation and increasingly by diversification). The marketing of "old" products on the international market then has usually two functions to perform: firstly, if demand declines as a result of structural, trade cycle- or market-related changes, and capacities built up in the home country are consequently underused, then exports can take up some of the slack[4]; secondly it is the idea of growth and reaction to the activities of the competition which stimulate companies to secure for themselves a market position in foreign countries, not just by export activities, but also by licensing deals or direct investment. It is precisely this second aspect which leads companies simultaneously to regard the "new markets" from the strategic point of view, and to their being prepared to take the peculiarities of these markets into account and to react to special conditions by appropriate adjustments to their sales packages. And so it happens that not just unchanged products are marketed, but also to some extent products which have been quite clearly changed, and this can on occasions lead to decisions which take on the character of a diversification.

The significance of strategies of market penetration and product policy expansion on international markets shows up under two aspects; firstly, once the actual choice of foreign market has been made one faces decisions about further developments on this market and secondly, there is now an altered point of view, such as is typical for multinational companies, and this is now a global one rather than one related to the country of origin. When one considers the partnership model of foreign trade and the scope of global decisions, International Marketing must not allow itself to be constrained by the limited point of view of companies which act according to the traditional

[4] To some extent therefore, decisions concerning internationalisation are in competition with other possibilities of market expansion, which might be realised by a more exact analysis of and appeal to additional customer groups in the home country, by means of for example segmentation and differentiation strategies.

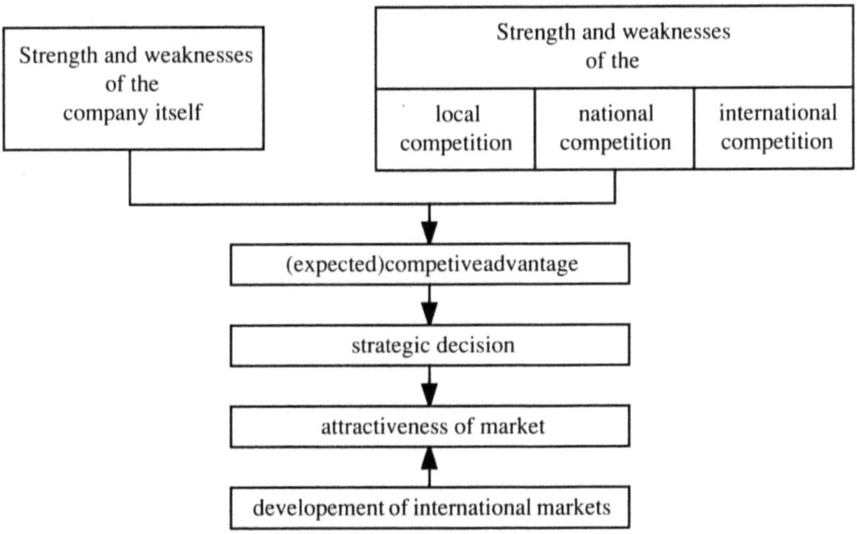

Diagram 17. Factors influencing international strategic decisions[5]

foreign trade patterns and think in terms of the home country, but must encompass the totality of strategic decisions.

In addition to market factors and an analysis of a company's own strengths and weaknesses, decisions in International Marketing must also always have regard to the strengths and weaknesses of national and international competition (Diagram 17).

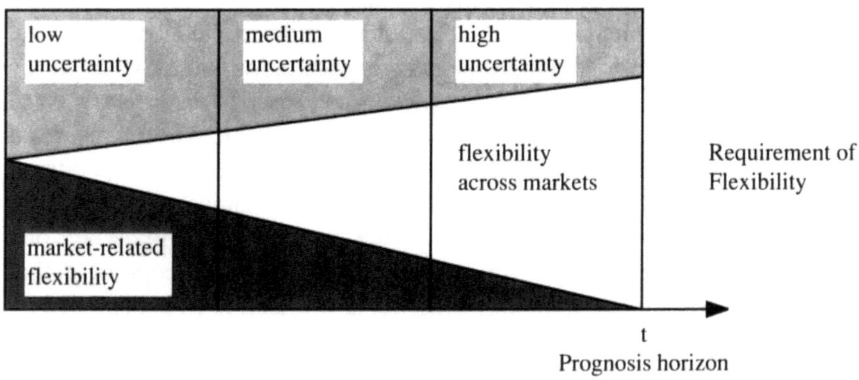

Diagram 18. Company flexibility and strategic planning[6]

[5] Diagram based on Aaker, D. A., Strategic Market Management, New York, 1984, p. 124.
[6] Cf. Meffert, H., Größere Flexibilität als Unternehmungskonzept, in: ZfbF, Vol. 37, No. 2 (Feb. 1985), p. 134.

The structuring of Strategic International Marketing always takes place too against a background of an increasing requirement of flexibility. The higher the degree of uncertainty becomes and the further in the future the planning horizon is set, the greater the requirement of flexibility becomes. This requirement of flexibility is no longer, or only to a very limited extent, dependent on the given market conditions, but is strongly marked by the expected market developments and structures (Diagram 18). With their international strategies Japanese companies are increasingly according primacy to flexibility. They strive for a mixture of export and import deals, of local production and component supply, of licensing deals and joint ventures. The mixture of these various types of foreign activity provides Japanese companies with a high degree of flexibility, so that they are thereby able to adjust themselves to the changing conditions in which they operate, whether these are subject to economics, trade policy, or exchange rates.

2. International Product Life-Cycle Analyses

The analysis of product life-cycle is an essential methodological element of Strategic International Marketing.

The model of the product life-cycle distinguishes the phases of the introduction, growth, maturity and decline (Diagram 19). The profit threshold is not normally crossed until the growth phase, and even during the phase of

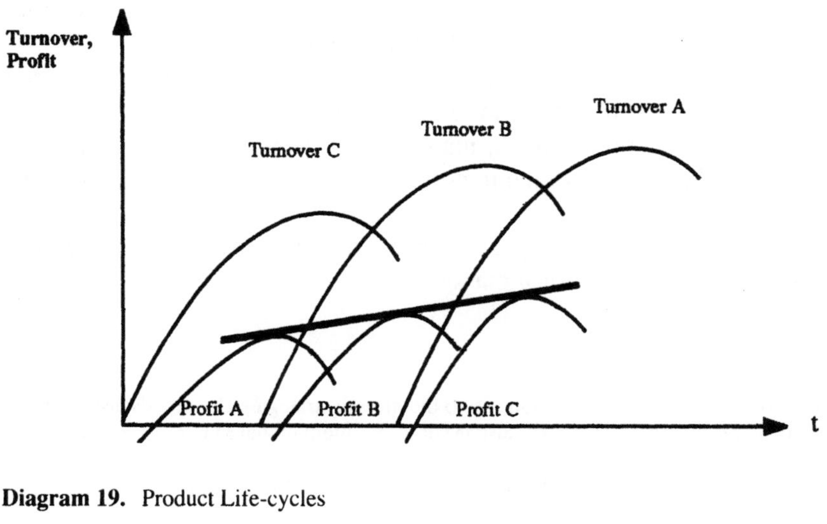

Diagram 19. Product Life-cycles

maturity the profit comes once more under pressure. This forces companies to find new markets for their present products or to bring new products onto the market.[7]

The product life-cycle must be seen under the aspect of increasing market saturation and growing international competition, and also with reference to the introduction onto the market of new products, brands or services. This leads to the necessity of undertaking a worldwide analysis of the product life-cycle.

The theory of international exchange relationships makes increasing use of product life-cycle in order to explain international trade currents.[8] From the product life-cycle there is derived a trade cycle, which passes through four characteristic stages:

Stage 1: Export strength of the German (or American or Japanese) company.
Stage 2: Production is started up in other countries, especially the previously importing countries.
Stage 3: The new product becomes increasingly competitive on third markets and gains increasing shares of them.
Stage 4: Traditional national production comes under increasing import pressure from the products manufactured abroad.

This model of the course of events is extremely characteristic of the development of the world economy. It can be observed with investment goods (such as steel, chemical products, or in shipbuilding) with consumer goods (such as motor vehicles or entertainment electronics) and with services.

Within the framework of their international strategic decisions companies are therefore called upon to analyse the position of their products and services in this process of change, in order to make subsequent decisions concerning the consideration of individual foreign markets, the market exploitation strategies, or the creation of a standardised supply policy.

The concept of the product life-cycle with the characteristic new product developments must be placed in an international framework. The separate phases of introduction, growth, maturity and decline are for this purpose differentiated according to the important actual and potential sales markets (Table 21).

This matrix, proposed by Leontiades, outlines three typical life-cycle constellations in international markets:

[7] Here one notices the close relationship to the growth strategies already discussed, which correspond to the Ansoff matrix; see also: Majaro, S., International Marketing, London 1977, p. 82.

[8] Cf. Terpstra, V., International Marketing, 3rd.Edn., Chicago 1983,.pp. 30 ff.

Table 21. Different stages in the product life-cycle worldwide[9]

Countries \ Stages	Introduction	Growth	Maturity	Decline
West Germany		y	z	x
EC Countries	y	z	x	
USA and Japan	y	z		x
OPEC States		zx		
COMECON Countries	xz			
Developing Countries	z	x		

Product X is taken to refer to a product which is in the phase of decline on the West German market as the result of market saturation, technological obsolescence or international competition, for example colour television sets. A comparable market fate is to be recorded for the USA and Japan, whereas in the markets of the member-states of the EC a high volume of turnover is still being attained although without any rate of increase. In the OPEC states and the developing countries on the other hand there is by contrast a quite pronounced growth situation, whereas introduction into the Comecon states is only just beginning.

The assessment of international market opportunities always requires too that estimates be made of the potential volumes of the individual markets or of the various groups of countries. The market shares for consumer goods in the Comecon countries will, for structural reasons, not attain the volume of those of EC member states, and also the sales possibilities of the large number of developing countries are dependent upon the restrictive trade policies of these countries and on their debt situation. Therefore one cannot expect the product life-cycle observed in one country to repeat itself in exactly the same form (at a later point in time) in another country, but one must rather take a realistic view of the environmental conditions which influence the market potential in both absolute and relative measure.

Product Y refers to a product which is in the phase of maturity, exhibiting high turnover figures, on the West German market, as in the case with the various models of the motor vehicle manufacturers. In other countries the same vehicle type is only in the growth phase and in some countries it is only in the introductory phase.

Product Z, finally, refers to a product in the growth phase, for example office computers. In some countries this product is only in the introductory phase, whereas in some markets it cannot be obtained at all.

---

[9] Cf. Leontiades, J., Multinational Corporate Strategy, Lexington/Mass., Toronto 1985, p. 76.

These internationally differing developments can be clearly determined in quantitative terms, so that precise foundations for planning can be derived from them. At the same time it may not be assumed that the development in all important sub-markets of the world will follow the same pattern. It is therefore necessary to analyse exactly the typical processes of development in the individual sub-markets and then to draw these into international comparisons as bases for decisions.

3. International Market and Development Prognoses

Whereas it is true that Strategic International Marketing decisions proceed from the actual situation and draw upon experiences from the past, they are primarily and principally oriented towards future events and developments. Here it is that specific uncertainty relating to future developments that lies at the root of the special methodological problems which accompany prognoses in the sphere of International Marketing decisions.

In order to bolster their International Marketing decisions companies must make systematic use of the techniques of prognosis which have been developed in various branches of knowledge. In this case it is necessary to make prognoses in the following areas, and then combine them all into a collective prognosis:

- development of the world economy
- economic, social and political development of individual countries and economic regions,
- development and worldwide distribution of certain products, services and technologies,
- development of individual companies and combinations of companies.

Each of the four areas of prognosis named is built in turn upon a variety of partial prognoses. Diagram 20 makes clear by way of an example how complex forecasts can be gained from a balanced combination of partial forecasts.

Prognoses rely to a large extent upon a transfer of empirical values from the past to the future. To this extent they rest either implicitly or explicitly upon assumptions about regularities which influence the content of the prognosis. If, for example, one plots the growth of a specific size G against a temporal axis, then various growth curves can be obtained.

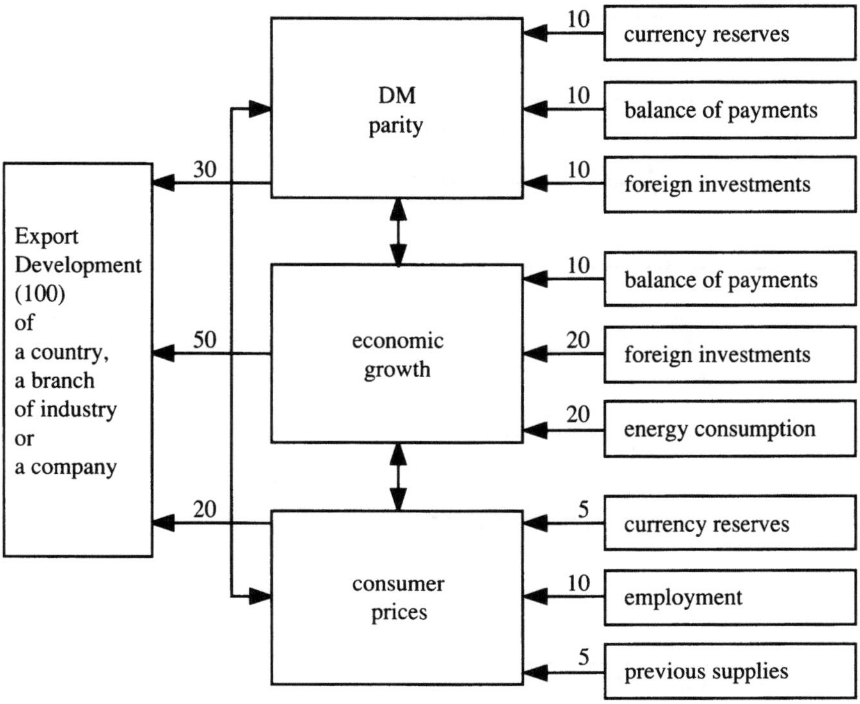

Diagram 20. The structure of prognosis construction in Strategic International Marketing[10]

For companies it is now a matter of interpreting the developments in the world economy and in the various potential foreign markets within the framework of such development graphs. The appropriate prognosis models may be extrapolations of trends, regression analyses, Delphi models or other processes. One can in principle distinguish here between quantitative and qualitative methods of prognosis. Quantitative methods are especially suitable if the regularity which has been ascertained is amenable to mathematical-statistical analysis. In particular they produce good results when used with such prognoses as exhibit only a limited temporal horizon. Since they always abstract in a very thorough-going manner from the complexity of real events they may only be used in a context of all other things being equal, but then if the marginal conditions change – and this is typical of, for example, structural change – then mistakes arise in the prognoses. To this extent therefore, as the

[10] Taken from: Meissner, H. G., Entwicklungsperspektiven des internationalen Marketing: Zukünftige Szenarien und Meßprobleme, in: Meffert, H. (Ed.), Marketing im Wandel, Wiesbaden 1980, p. 176.

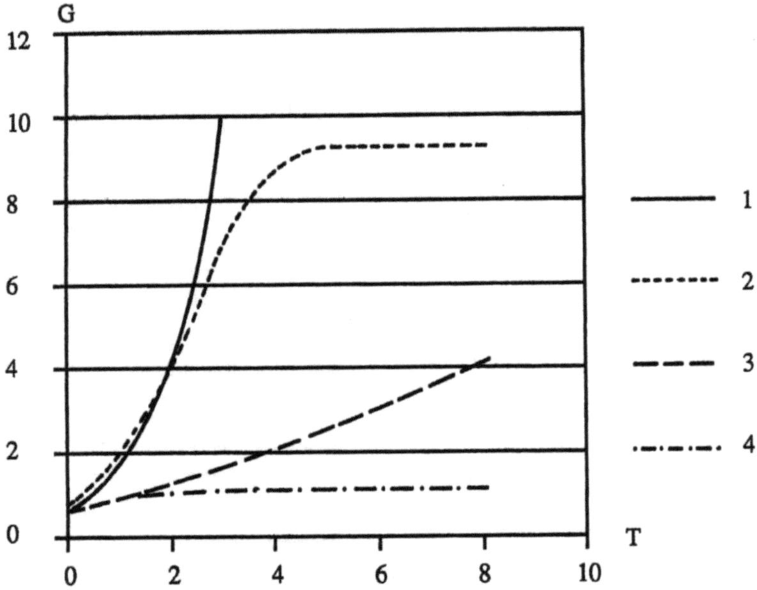

Diagram 21. Examples of growth curves[11]

Degree of difficulty and temporal horizon of the forecasts	Methods most suitably employed
long-term(5–20 years high degree of difficulty medium-term (2–5 years) medium degree of difficulty short-term (1 year) low degree of difficulty	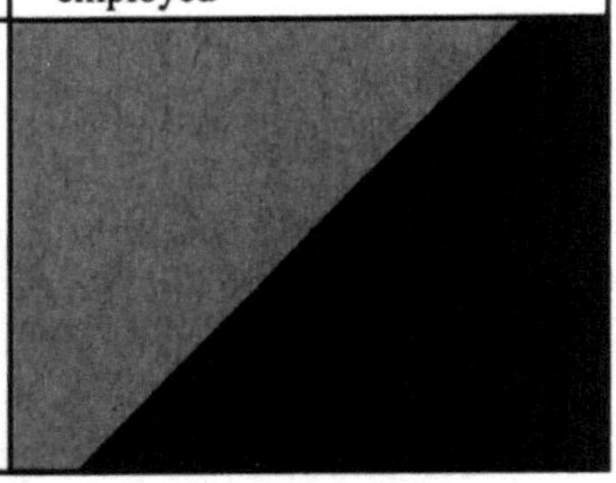

qualitative methods — quantitative methods

Diagram 22. Temporal horizon and methods of prognosis[12]

temporal horizon increases and in cases of structural change the qualitative prognosis techniques gain in significance (Diagram 22).

The interpretation of long-term developments takes place with the aid of the scenario technique. This is a matter of interpreting future developments in a logical and probable interrelationship. Scenarios do not restrict themselves

[11] Taken from: Kahn, H., World Economic Development, New York 1979, p. 505.
[12] Taken from: Meissner, H. G., Außenhandels-Marketing, Stuttgart 1981, p. 57.

to the development of individual phenomena, but take overall developments as their field of attention. Such scenarios are developed using, for example, the Delphi method, and they are often formulated as alternative scenarios, as may be seen in the following examples of air traffic prognosis up to the year 2,000 (Table 22). Scenario O represents the optimum variant, Scenario M the medium alternative and Scenario P the pessimistic expectation.

Table 22. Scenarios on the example of air traffic prognosis[13]

Scenario O.

- Steady improvement in political and economic cooperation, reduction in political tensions.
- Slow reduction in economic difficulties, of population increase and of gaps in energy supply.
- Great advances in synthetic fuel and fusion technologies.
- Slowly increasing demand for transport.
- Marked increase in company efficiency.
- Moderate replacements in air fleet with high financial costs.
- Generally sufficient supply of fuel with occasional interruptions.
- Steady improvement in tariff coordination and in multilateral regulation of tariff laws.
- Company profits in general, with well-managed organisations, clearly higher than increasing company costs.

Scenario M.

- Moderately successful international coordination; persistent political tensions, a few regional wars.
- Persistence of protectionism, of the population increase and of gaps in energy supply.
- Some advances in synthetic fuel and fusion technologies.
- Stagnating demand for transport.
- Slow increase in company efficiency.
- Minor replacements in air fleet, with sometimes extremely high financial costs.
- Occasional shortages and rationing of fuel in some regions.
- Slow advances in tariff coordination and in the regulation of traffic laws.
- Company profits just about sufficient to cover sharply increasing company costs.

Scenario P

- Collapse of the international order; increasing political tensions and regional wars.
- Increasing protectionism; unchecked population growth; critical disimprovement of the economic position in the developing countries.
- Far-reaching crises of energy supply; delayed development in synthetic fuel technology; no developement in fusion technology.
- Decreasing demand for transport.
- Stagnating company efficiency; in many places a persistently bad utilisation of airspace.
- Practical stagnation in replacements of air fleet.
- Extensive shortfall and rationing of fuel.
- Collapse of tariff co-ordination and of efforts towards a multilateral regulation of traffic law.
- Many companies make heavy losses; reductions and close-downs of companies.

[13] Example taken from: Guldimann, W., Luftverkehr an der Jahrtausendwende, in: Neue Züricher Zeitung, No. 7 of 11.01.1983, p. 23.

4. Early Warning Systems

Specially developed early warning systems are an important prognosis instrument employed by International Marketing. Early warning systems deal with quantities of influence which are systematically perceived and evaluated, and which in the course of events precede later developments.[14] Such early warning systems have been developed for particular countries. They play a role in the choice of foreign markets and particularly in decisions about foreign investments.

The strategic choice of specific foreign markets takes place according to a scheme of action, which is intented to lead ultimately to a fine analysis and the final selection of countries. Whereas the selection of export markets is carried out according to indicators such as buying power and the distribution of buying power, there are also indicators of further economic development of which the following are examples:[15]

- number of inhabitants per square kilometer,
- gross social product per inhabitant,
- number of telephones per inhabitant,
- kilometers of railway track per inhabitant,
- cars per inhabitant.

Early warning systems have attained special importance in the assessment of country risks which must be taken into consideration by banks in deciding their credit policy and by companies when making decisions about foreign investments. Worthy of note in this context is for example the BERI (Business Environment Risk Index) which has been drawn up for the various countries of the world (Table 23). Based on evaluation by experts and proceeding by way of a point evaluation system, the BERI arrives at a statement concerning the country-specific character of the risk with respect to various investment criteria.

The BERI links up various determining factors of the investment climate of a country, such as political stability, inflation, balance of payments, economic development, availability of skilled workers, available financial means etc. – altogether 15 factors – which are evaluated on a scale of 0 to 4 with decimal subdivision (0 = unacceptable conditions, 4 = very good conditions for investment), with an additional weighting of the significance of these factors (thus the number of points gains a threefold weighting in the case of political stability, and half the result again of the point evaluation if skilled

---

[14] Cf. Reichmann, T., Controlling mit Kennzahlen, Munich 1985, p. 88.
[15] Cf. Kulhavy, E., Internationales Marketing, Linz 1981, pp. 85 ff.

Table 23. Examples of the BERI[16]

Investment criteria	West Germany	Brazil	Italy	India	Nigeria	United Kingdom	USA
Political stability: the likelihood of sudden political upheaval and its effect on business life and the climate of investment	3,1	2,9	1,3	1,8	1,7	2,6	3,7
Attitude towards foreign investors and profits: general assent to the principles of the market economy and the extent to which the costs of social advance are laid upon private industry	3,2	3,0	1,9	1,4	2,2	2,9	3,3
Nationalisation: the spectrum from appropriation without compensation to the preferential treatment of nationals	3,5	2,9	2,2	1,3	2,0	2,2	3,7
Monetary devaluation: the consequences of monetary devaluation and effective measures to reduce the consequences of inflation for the conduct of business	3,3	1,6	1,4	1,5	1,8	1,2	2,3
Balance of payments: the balance of payments of current accounts and of capital costs, as well as their influence on the transferability of the holdings of foreign investors	3,4	1,7	1,1	1,3	2,8	1,1	2,4
Bureaucracy: general tempo and efficiency of the civil service; also in regard to such matters as the processing of customs formalities; foreign exchange transfers and similar tasks	2,8	1,9	1,4	1,2	1,5	2,2	3,1
Economic growth: long-term economic growth of real GNP in stages of 3%, 3% to 6%, 6% to 10% and above 10%	2,8	2,8	1,4	1,5	2,8	1,3	2,4
Convertibility of currency: the ease with which the national currency can be converted into foreign currency, and the assessment of the currency on the exchange market	3,6	2,1	1,9	1,0	2,5	2,0	3,9
Implementation of contracts: the extent to which contracts are recognised, and any difficulties which might arise from differences in language and mentality	3,3	2,2	1,9	1,6	1,8	3,1	3,0
Wages and productivity: item costs with regard to wages, ancillary wage costs, work productivity and attitudes to work	2,9	2,2	1,6	1,8	1,5	1,5	2,5
Availability of experts and services: the support which a company can expect in the areas of accountancy, legal advice, marketing advice, technology and building construction	3,2	2,5	2,0	2,0	1,5	2,7	3,5
Communications and transport: the quality of transport and communications facilities within the country and between company headquaters and branch plants	3,6	2,3	2,0	1,7	1,3	2,8	3,9
Local management and partners: quality and number of nationals who can participate in higher level management or who can make their own capital available	3,1	2,4	2,0	1,8	1,7	2,7	3,6
Short-term credits: general availability of short-term credits to companies in foreign ownership and the possibility of investing money for short periods	3,0	1,8	1,6	1,3	2,5	2,4	3,0
Long-term credits and own capital: availability of and conditions for long-term capital in the local currency as loans or as own capital	3,0	1,8	1,6	1,3	2,5	2,5	3,0
compensated total points:	79,4	58,2	41,0	36,7	52,6	53,6	78,5

Key to the point system: 4 = very favourable ; 3 = good ; 2= satisfactory 1 = bad ; 0 = unsupportable

[16] Taken from: Meffert, H., Althans, J., Internationales Marketing, Stuttgart 1982, p. 79.

Table 24. Scoring process for the obtaining of risk indices[17]

	Weighting $N_i=n_j=100$ (1)	Probabilities: favourable development (2)	Probabilities: unfavourable development (3)	weighted probabilities: favourable development (4)	weighted probabilities: unfavourable development (5)	Risk Indicator (4–5)
Political Factors 25						
– Army upheaval	12	0,25	0,15	3,0	1,8	+1,2
– Labour conflict	3	0,0	0,3	0,0	0,9	-0,9
– Strength of armed extremist groups	6	0,0	0,1	0,0	0,6	-0,6
– Government stability	4	0,2	0,0	0,8	0,0	+0.8
						+0,5
Economic Factors 45						
– Inflation	15	0,0	0,5	0,0	7,5	-7,5
– Gross National Product	10	0,25	0,0	2,5	0,0	+2,5
– Effect of financial programmes	3	0,3	0,2	0,9	0,6	+0,3
– Agricultural production	4	0,6	0,1	2,4	0,4	+2,0
– Industrial production	5	0,2	0,0	1,0	0,0	+1,0
– Gross domestic investment	3	0,3	0,0	0,9	0,0	+0,9
– Balance of trade	5	0,45	0,0	2,25	0,0	+2,25
						+1,45
Financial Factors 30						
– Balance of payments	12	0,15	0,05	1,8	0,6	+0,6
– Foreign currency reserves	5	0,15	0,0	0,75	0,0	+0,75
– Foreign debts	3	0,0	0,45	0,0	1,35	-1,35
– Meat exports	3	0,2	0,0	0,6	0,0	+0,6
– Grain exports	3	0,3	0,0	0,9	0,0	+0,9
– Foreign investments	4	0,2	0,0	0,8	0,0	+0,8
						+2,9
Risk factor:						= +4,85

As a positive value results, a somewhat favourable development may be expected, i.e. the risk is not estimated as being very high.

[17] Taken from: Dworak, B. M., Das Länderrisiko als bankbetriebliches Problem, Berlin 1985, p. 139.

workers are available). The best investment climate is indicated by the maximum attainable value of 100 points.[18] The banks, business periodicals and international company advisers have developed similar systems for the early recognition of country risks.[19] Thus the banks have drawn up a scoring process for determining the risk indices of individual countries on the basis of probabilities (Table 24).[20]

The volume of international debt has grown in significance as an early indicator in assessing country risk.[21] The import capability of a country, its payment capability for the transfer of dividends, licence fees and capital repayments, as well as the payment of interest on and repayment of international credit already granted all depend on the extent of the international debt which a country has already incurred. A drop in the import quota and an exhaustion of foreign investment entail severe economic problems for the countries concerned, e.g. those of Latin America, and it then becomes highly probable that these will lead to social and political tensions and crisis situations.

5. International Comparisons and Analogies

The various countries show characteristic differences in the development of demand for investment and consumer goods, for products and services. Certain aspects of consumer behaviour are, for example, typically Japanese or typically German – let us say the demand for sake in Japan or the demand for beer in Germany.It is precisely the consumer habits of the various countries which make the existing cultural differences particularly clear.[22]

The international differentiation of demand depends not just on cultural factors, but also on the buying power which the population in the country concerned has attained. The income per head of individual countries is an

---

[18] Cf. Welge, M., Management in deutschen multinationalen Unternehmungen, Stuttgart 1980, p. 338.
[19] Cf. Berekoven, L., Internationales Marketing, 2nd. Edn., Herne and Berlin 1985, p. 113.
[20] Cf. Cramer, M., Das internationale Kreditgeschäft der Banken, Wiesbaden 1981, p. 154.
[21] Cf. Meissner, H. G., Singer, H., Jahn, W., Banning, Th. E., Die internationale Verschuldung als Problem der Unternehmensführung, Vol. 237 of the Wissenschaftliche Arbeitsgemeinschaft für Technik und Wirtschaft des Landes Nordrhein-Westfalen, Dortmund 1985.
[22] Cf. Meissner, H. G., Systemvergleich zwischen deutschen und japanischen Marktstrategien, in: Gaugler, E., Meissner, H. G., Thom, N. (Eds.), Zukunftsaspekte der anwendungsorientierten Betriebswirtschaftslehre, Stuttgart 1986, pp. 211–222 and Meissner, H. G., Japanische und deutsche Marketingstrategien: Ein struktureller Vergleich, in: Mitteilungen der Bundesstelle für Außenhandelsinformation, November 1985.

important indicator of the demand potential. However, the average per head income does not of itself say anything about the distribution of income. In developing countries above all, but also in modern industrial countries, we often find a very varied distribution of income between the ruling elites, the middle classes and ordinary workers, whereas in other countries (for example in Scandinavia) we may observe a levelling-out of income. In addition to this individual countries often exhibit extremely large differences with respect to income and consumption between the large cities and the agricultural areas.

Nevertheless, world-political and world-economic developments have also led to the development of similarities in consumption patterns internationally.[23]

These international similarities in consumption owe their existence not least to the increased and simplified processes of international communication and information exchange. These give rise to international processes of learning which show themselves in, among other things,the standardisation of patterns of consumption. To this extent it is precisely the orientation towards the lifestyles of foreign cultures which is at the present time reducing the significance of national consumer habits and allowing international consumer habits to arise. The occasion for this is often provided by wishes to identify with other peoples and nations – even if this identification only takes place in the sphere of lemonade or of fast food restaurants.

Table 25. The dynamics of international structures of demand and consumption patterns

Changes in factors of influence in the national context / Changes in factors of influence in international comparison	International differentiation	International standardisation
1 **Income Per Head** : rising : stagnating : falling		
2 **Social Stratification and Income Distribution** : equitable : non-equitable		
3 **Town and Country Distribution** : urban culture : rural culture : mixed types		

[23] Cf. Berekoven, L., Internationale Verbrauchsangleichung, Nuremberg 1977.

The task facing Strategic International Marketing is therefore to analyse the differentiation and also the international standardisation of consumer habits and to interpret the dynamic of consumer behaviour against the background of income development and social structure (Table 25).

A relevant analysis indicates countries, in which the rising income per head makes possible a clear adjustment towards consumption patterns in internationally leading countries (Table 26) e.g. with reference to the demand for cars or for house furnishings. At the same time, however, in some countries and in some consumer goods sectors there has been witnessed a reawakening of traditional values, despite rising income per head. Such a development is typical of, for example, the Republic of Korea.[24]

Table 26. National Product of selected countries in 1988[25]

Country	in DM (thousands of millions)	in DM per inhabitant
USA	11650	47300
Canada	1150	44500
Switzerland	270	40700
Norway	160	38800
Luxembourg	15	37900
Sweden	300	35500
West Germany	2120	34500
Japan	4260	34500
Denmark	170	33100
France	1850	33100
Great Britain	1840	32200
Italy	1830	31700
Netherlands	460	31200
Belgium	300	31200
Austria	230	30300
Spain	850	21800
Ireland	70	19400
Greece	170	16600
Portugal	160	16600

International comparisons are especially important for marketing decisions if prognoses are required concerning the development of individual markets. Thus, for example, comparative studies are carried out of the furnishing of households with certain long-life consumer goods, such as e.g. TV sets (Diagram 23).

[24] Cf. Korean Overseas Information Service (Eds.), A Handbook of Korea, 4th Edn., Seoul 1982, p. 480 and pp. 325 ff.

[25] All figures are estimates taken from: Institut der deutschen Wirtschaft (Eds.), Zahlen zur wirtschaftlichen Entwicklung der Bundesrepublik Deutschland 1989, Cologne 1989.

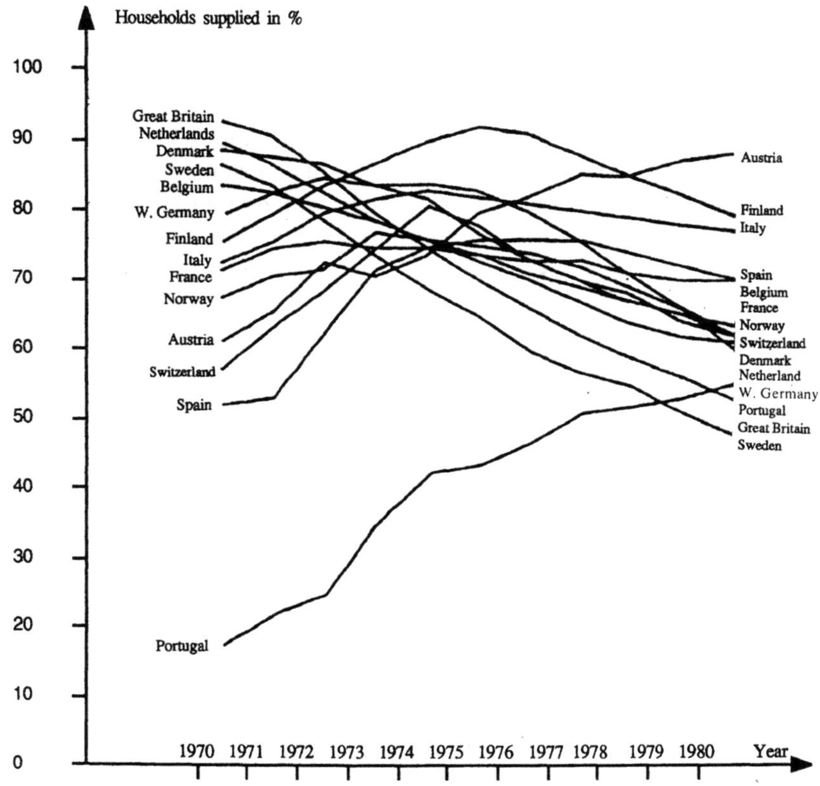

Diagram 23. Availability of black and white television sets in various countries[26]

Such comparative studies, carried out across various countries and with the time dimension kept in mind represent an important and frequently employed instrument of prognosis in International Marketing. An underlying supposition here is that certain developments in demand may be seen to emerge in various countries but with some time lapse, so that companies gain the opportunity of reinforcing their International Marketing decisions by **deductions made from analogy**. With regard to the value of such analogies it is always essential to choose indicators on which proper deductions may be based. One may conclude , for example, that the structure of demand in West Germany in 1985 corresponds to that of Switzerland about ten years ago, as the present-day income per head of West Germany corresponds to the income per head of Switzerland ten years ago. From this example it is not difficult to see that the use of the income per head indicator is only sensible in the case of

[26] Taken from: Berekoven, L., Internationales Marketing, 2nd. Edn., Herne and Berlin 1985, p. 83.

some markets, whereas for others (e.g. black and white television sets in Diagram 23) it would lead to altogether senseless conclusions. For prognoses within the EC one might for example assume that the development of income in a country such as Spain will in 10–15 years time correspond to the income situation at present prevailing in West Germany. Thus the structure of demand in Spain around the turn of the millennium may – and in some cases undoubtedly will – correspond to those in the West Germany of 1985. The basis of such prognoses is the expectation that as the income per head rises those countries which are at present less advanced in their development will grow into those patterns of consumption and demand which has already been actualised in earlier years by other countries.

However, such international analogies neglect the national and regional differences and thereby the sociocultural particularities of individual countries. Furthermore such analogies take equally little account of the technological changes which occur in the meantime, and the changes of values which the individual societies may undergo. For these reasons there can be no simple, undifferentiated transfer of the developments in demand from one country to another country at some future period.

However international comparisons are not just of interest only if one represents future developments on the time axis, but regression analyses are also gaining in significance. One possibility here is to demonstrate how the possession of specific products is related to per head income, e.g. the development of car density with respect to income in various countries (Diagram 24).

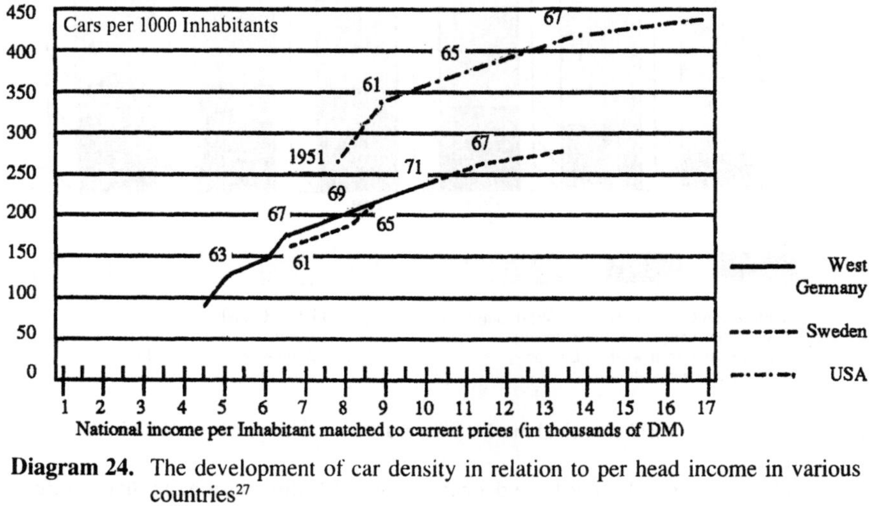

Diagram 24. The development of car density in relation to per head income in various countries[27]

[27] Taken from: Lewandowski, R., Prognose- und Informationssysteme, Vol. 1, Berlin und New York 1974, p. 385.

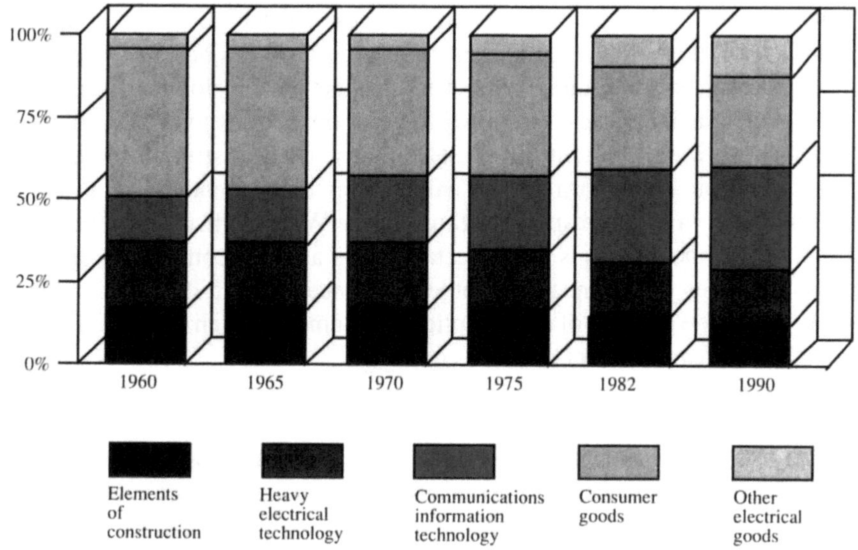

Diagram 25. Electrotechnical sub-markets[28] (in real terms with prices of 1982 in %)

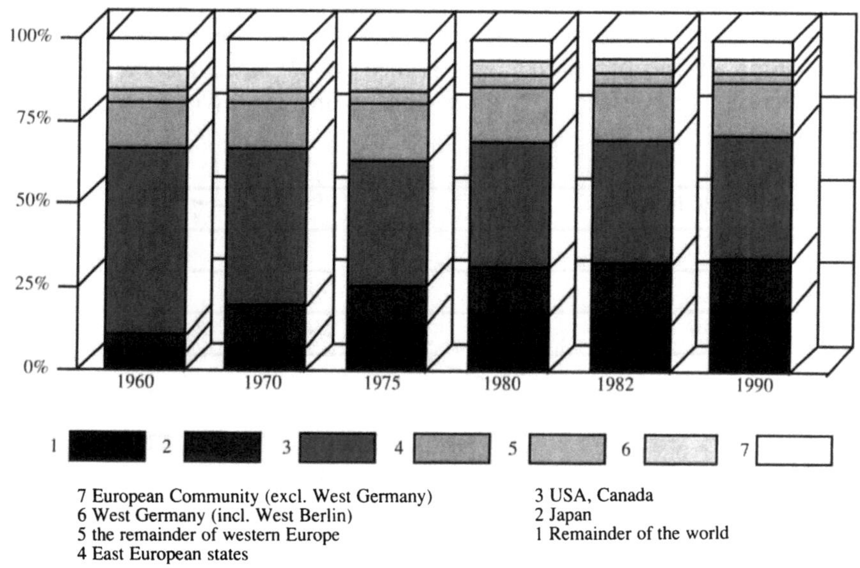

Diagram 26. The world electrical market[29] (in real terms with prices of 1982 in %)

[28] Taken from: Plettner, B., Zur Lage der europäischen Elektroindustrie, in: Siemens Zeitschrift, Vol. 58, No. 2, 1984, p. 6.

[29] Taken from: Plettner, B., Zur Lage der europäischen Elektroindustrie, in: Siemens Zeitschrift, Vol. 58, No. 2, 1984, p. 5.

Within the context of international comparisons it is important for companies in the various sectors, e.g. in the electrical industry, in the vehicle industry, or in the iron and steel industry to make a prognosis of the development of the individual technical sub-markets and to estimate the share which the individual regions of the world market will have in this market development. In such prognoses, one may discern relative displacements against the background of technological development and the shifting of commercial emphases owing to variations in the development of the world market.

According to details supplied by Siemens AG, the prognosis concerning the technical sub-markets in the electrical sector may be illustrated as shown in Diagram 25.

The prognosis for the world electrical market is based on the following development shown in Diagram 26.

6. Portfolio Analyses

The portfolio method has become the central instrument of strategic company management.[30] Portfolio analysis is intended to enable companies to arrive at a balancing of the long-term risks and opportunities. But the opening of portfolios also and very importantly makes it possible for companies to establish priorities for their decisions, e.g. priorities in the development of new technologies or in the opening-up of new markets.

Such portfolios are also of decisive importance for Strategic International Marketing. Companies active in international markets must concern themselves above all with the establishment of priorities in the choice of market, the determining of strategies to be employed in the opening of markets and also the provisions for abandoning sub-markets in the world economy, whether this be for commercial, technological or political reasons.

Secondly it is essential for companies to determine with what selection of their products or services they wish to become active and in which markets. For example, competitiveness can only be maintained on the markets of the USA or Japan if the products which are offered embody the most modern and at the same time the most mature technology. Markets in various developing countries must on the other hand be offered an appropriate technology, which

[30] Cf. Hahn, D., Taylor, B. (Eds.), Strategische Unternehmensplanung, 3rd Edn., Würzburg, Vienna 1984, pp. 49 ff and Hinterhuber, H. H., Strategische Unternehmungsführung, 3rd. Edn., Berlin and New York 1984, pp. 96 ff.

Table 27. Areas of portfolio analysis in International Marketing[31]

Activities / Areas	Analysis	Forecast	Assessment	Decision
Present state of	x			
foreign activities				
Country portfolio		x		
Product portfolio		x	x	
Relative competitive		x	x	
advantages			x	
Strategic goals and				
choice of strategy				
Strategic goal				x
portfolio (with				
allocation of				
resources)				

takes the special production and environmental conditions of these countries into account.

Thirdly , companies must decide upon the strategies which they wish to employ in the individual sub- markets and countries. There are several countries which are best treated by the traditional methods of export business and this often applies e.g. to the member states of the EC and other neighbouring European countries. By contrast, other countries demand that foreign investments take the form of joint ventures (as is the case in, for example, a number of developing countries) or the making of contracts of co-operation and of reciprocal business arrangements with the state trade countries.

The formulation of strategies in International Strategic Marketing requires a systematic and explicit operating procedure, in which phases and steps may be distinguished as shown by Table 27.

In a first step, the choice of foreign markets is carried out by weighting the risks in the various actual and potential markets.[32] This weighting can be undertaken with the aid of a point evaluation system and presented in the form of a polarity profile (Diagram 27).

Weightings are drawn up on the basis of the targets set and the experiences of the companies, and they allow for the varying significances of the individual risks. With reference to risk intensity, it is necessary to bear in mind not just the relation between various alternatives, but also their absolute significance in the sense of critical levels. If a certain critical risk level (e.g. 0.7 for

[31] The concept is taken from: Hinterhuber, H. H., Strategische Unternehmungsführung, 3rd. Edn., Berlin and New York 1984, pp. 94–95.
[32] Cf. Bernkopf, G., Strategien zur Auswahl ausländischer Märkte, Munich 1980, pp. 61 ff.

commercial risk in a developing country) is reached or surpassed, then market entry should not be considered unless special types of risk limitation measures should be available, perhaps within the context of a Hermes Credit Insurance.

In a second step a country matrix is drawn up, which plots the risk potential of individual markets against their market attractiveness (Diagram 28). The attractiveness of a foreign market consists mainly in the volume of demand, the business and development policy followed and the conditions of the sociocultural environment.

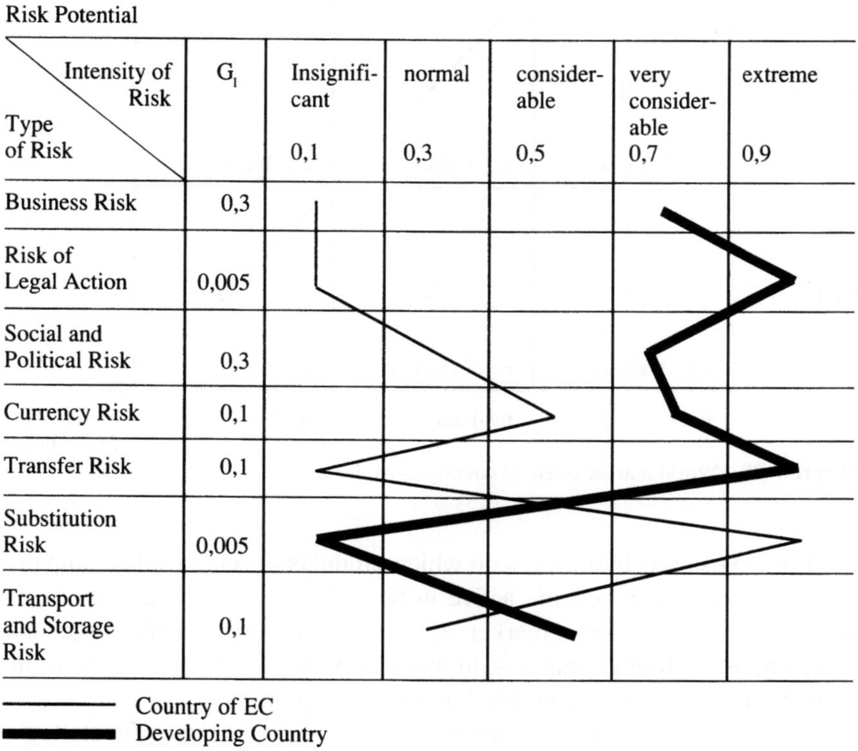

Rule for Making Decision:

[1] If one of the I risk intensities > 0,7, market entry is too risky.

[2] IF R_I ΣG_I 0,5, market entry is too risky

Diagram 27. Analysis of country risk[33]

[33] Taken from: Meffert, H., Althans, J., Internationales Marketing, Stuttgart 1982, p. 74.

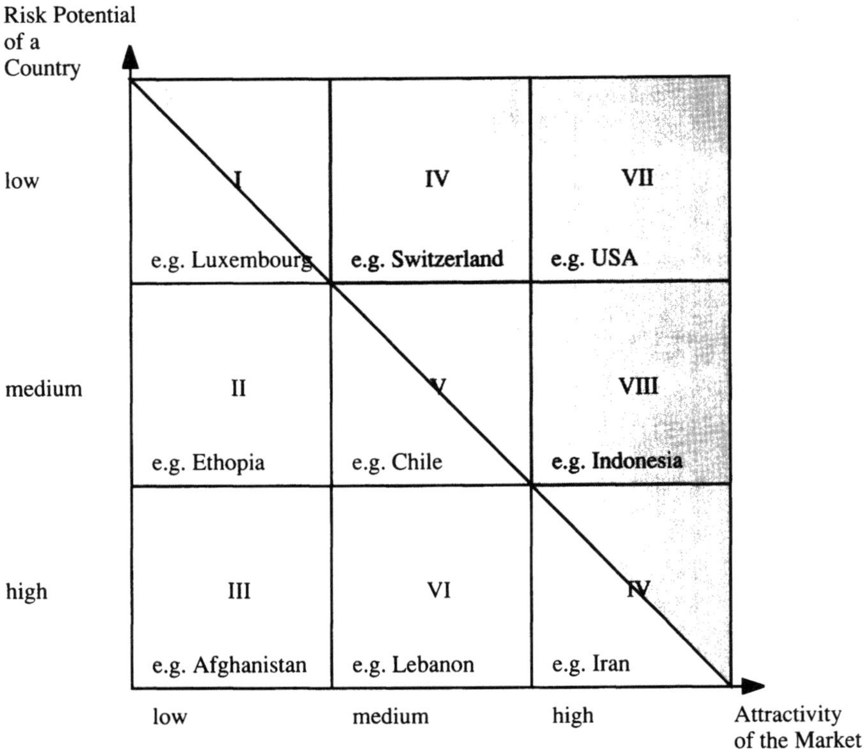

Diagram 28. World market-oriented country portfolio[34]

The next step is to decide with which products or services the company concerned wishes to become active in the individual countries. Here it is necessary to make a careful market segmentation, especially in the larger and more important foreign markets, in order to be in a position to exhaust the market potential in a differentiated manner (Diagram 29).[35]

In this context it is necessary to draw attention to a specific strategic procedure, which is oriented worldwide towards similar market segments. Here it is not the general country-specific market attractiveness which influences the decision for specific markets, but the recognition of the existence of similar structures of demand and similar consumer habits in segments (and perhaps only in small segments) of different markets. These may be explained especially by the international approximation of the lifesty-

[34] Meissner, H. G., Winkelgrund, R., Internationales Marketing als Herausforderung deutscher Unternehmen, in: Marketing, Vol. 4, No. 2 (May 1982), p. 117.
[35] Cf. Raffée, H., Segler, K., Marketingstrategien im Export, In: Dichtl, E., Issing, O. (Eds.), Exporte als Herausforderung für die deutsche Wirtschaft, Cologne 1984, pp. 297–307.

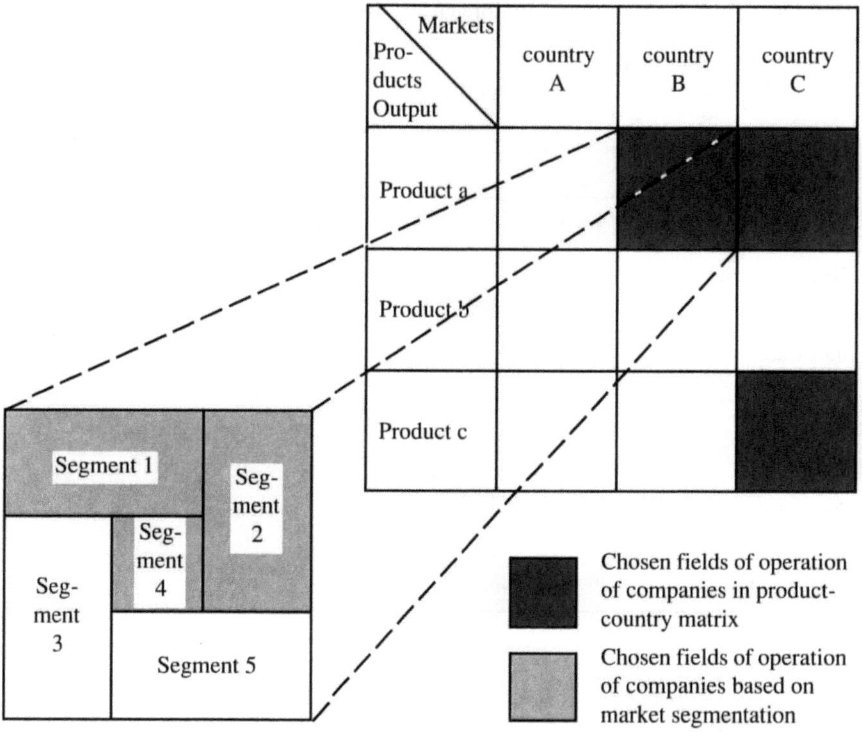

Diagram 29. Matrix for market selection in Strategic International Marketing[36]

les of certain population groups, and here may be seen the significance of lifestyles for International Marketing – in this case with respect to strategic aspects of market selection.[37]

Building on the product-country matrix, one then undertakes the appropriate choice of strategy for opening up, or further extending, the individual foreign markets. It is advisable in this process to construct, under the heading of risks and opportunities, a portfolio of various market approach strategies for different markets (Table 28).

A typical difficulty for Strategic International Marketing consists in the compression of these three different aspects, namely the country, the product and the strategy portfolios into a single strategic portfolio (see Diagram 30).

[36] Taken from: Meissner, H. G., So erobern Sie schwierige Märkte, in: Rationalisierungs-Kuratorium der Deutschen Wirtschaft (Ed.), Export Conference 1984, Düsseldorf 1984, p. 26.
[37] Cf. Banning, Th. E., Lebensstilorientierte Marketing-Theorie, Heidelberg 1987.

Table 28. Portfolio of strategies for foreign activities

Selection of Strategy / Selection of Market	Export	Foreign Investment	Other Transfer Processes
Europe			
Other industrial countries			
State trade countries			
Developing countries			
Threshold countries			
OPEC countries			

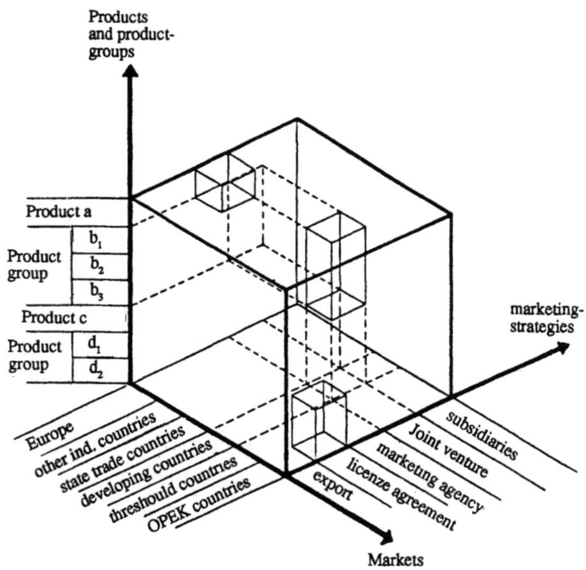

Diagram 30. Three-dimensional portfolio for Strategic International Marketing[38]

[38] Taken from Meissner, H. G., Winkelgrund, R., Internationales Marketing als Herausforderung deutscher Unternehmen, in: Marketing, Vol. 4, No. 2 (May 1982), p. 117.

Evaluation in the case of such portfolios is the result of a threefold process, and that is firstly by way of quantitative and qualitative **information**, which is procured by means of secondary research, secondly by way of the **experiences** which the companies have made, and finally by way of the **expectations** which the companies have with respect to the individual foreign markets. To this extent such portfolios represent a mixture of objective factors and subjective opinions.

For companies the core of the matter is to make transparent the opportunities and the risks of their foreign activities and to develop a convincing prognosis. This task can only be accomplished in a sensible manner so long as the companies remain conscious of the fundamental uncertainty and the risk which this entails. Sole recourse to quantitative data may reflect an only apparent exactitude, which does not in this form correspond to any reality, so that it is precisely quantitative exactness which can lead to ill-considered and wrong decisions.

7. The Management of Strategic Success Positions (SSP)

Within the framework of strategic management there has been developed a series of instruments which may be used both to assess and to provide a prognosis of the strategic success positions of individual companies. An important part is played in this contest by the PIMS analysis, which has been developed by the Strategic Planning Institute (SPI) in Cambridge, Massachusetts. The PIMS analysis ("Profit Impact of Market Strategies")[39] examines the influence of profit and especially of profit expectation on the marketing strategies of companies.

The PIMS programme is based on quantified details of individual companies and their fields of decision with reference to

- specific characteristics of the environments in which the company is active,
- competitive position,
- structure of the processes of production,
- efforts in research and development,
- marketing expenditure,

[39] Cf. Neubauer, F.F., Das PIMS-Programm und Portfolio-Management, in: Hahn, D., Taylor, B. (Eds.), Strategische Unternehmensplanung, 3rd Edn., Würzburg 1984, pp. 165–192.

– financial results of past performance (profit, cashflow)

and other relevant data.

On the basis of these data there is then obtained an optimum strategy for the company concerned. In deciding strategy the profitability of investment, the ROI ("Return on Investment") is assigned a decisive role.

An important further development of the PIMS concept is represented by the concept of the Management of Strategic Success Positions, as defined by Pümpin.

"A Strategic Sucess Position is a precondition, consciously created in a company by the construction of important and dominant capabilities, which allows a company to obtain long-term above-average results, by comparison with the competition."[40]

The underlying idea of the concepts of Strategic Success Positions is that companies concentrate on specific activities in the light of economic and historical development, while other areas of activity remain beyond their scope (Diagram 31).

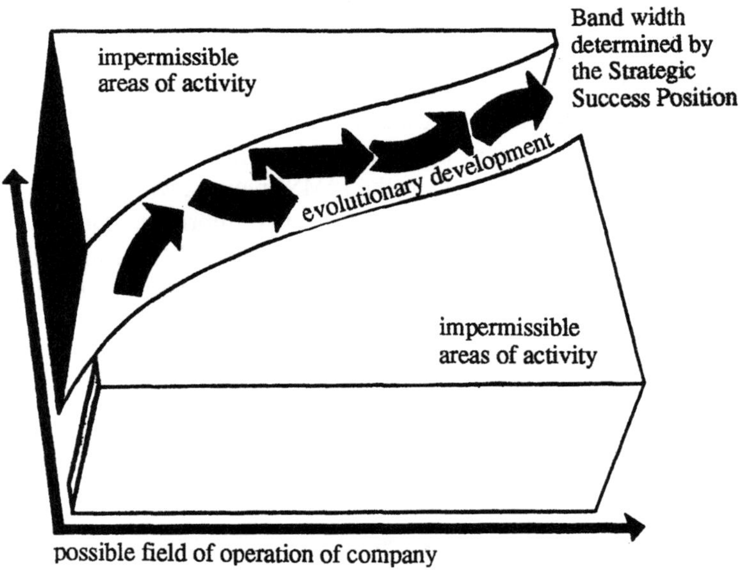

Diagram 31. Basic mechanism for the management of Strategic Success Positions[41]

[40] Pümpin, C., Management strategischer Erfolgspositionen, Berne and Stuttgart 1982, p. 34.
[41] Taken from: Pümpin, C., Management strategischer Erfolgspositionen, Berne and Stuttgart 1982, p. 41.

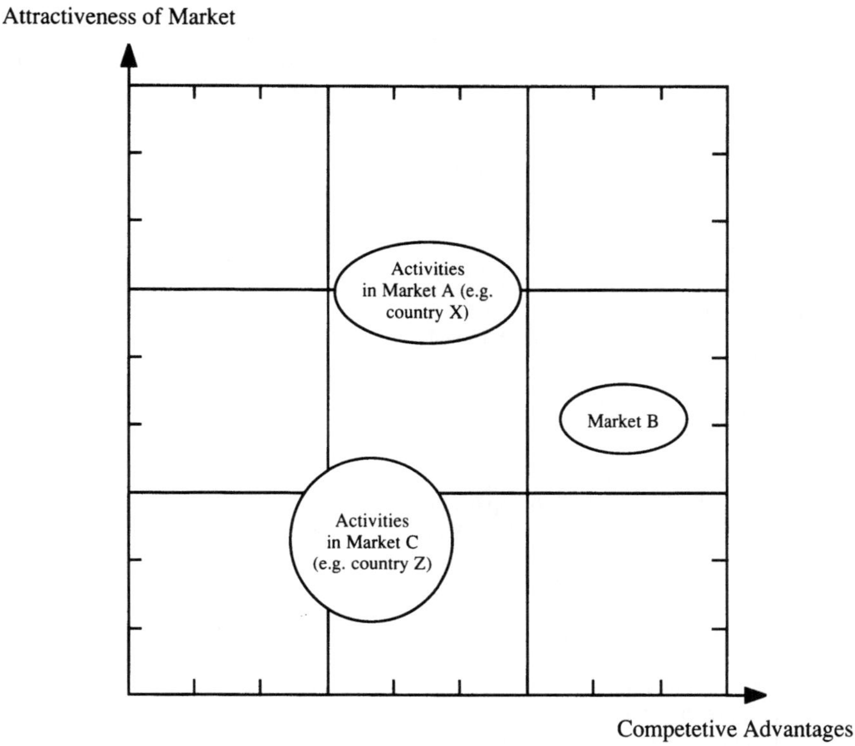

Diagram 32. Example of a market portfolio matrix for activities in countries A,B and C[42]

The SSP concept thereby combines portfolio analyses with analysis of the capabilities of companies. This combination plays a very significant part especially in the context of Strategic International Marketing, as this area is faced again and again with the task of identifying new market gaps in the world market, and thereby adjusting market activities in the various countries both to the specific capabilities of individual companies and to the environmental conditions of the individual sub-markets (Diagram 32).

Future-oriented capability analysis, which takes the present situation as starting-point and considers time-periods of 5,10 or 15 years, differentiates with respect to product-related,market-related and functional capabilities (Table 29).

[42] Taken from: Pümpin, C., Management strategischer Erfolgspositionen, Berne and Stuttgart 1982, p. 151.

Table 29. Capabilities analysis of a company[43]

Criteria	Present-day situation	t+5	t+10	t+15
1 Product-related capabilities				
– development, production and marketing Product Group A	+	+	-	0
– development, production and marketing Product Group B	-	0	+	+
– etc.				
2 Market-related capabilities				
– for the effective opening and exploitation of Market X	0	+	+	+
– for the effective opening and exploitation of Market Y	+	0	-	-
– etc.				
3 Functional capabilities				
– offering leading products of top quality	0	+	+	+
– offering a well-balanced product range	+	0	-	-
– providing first-class service	+	+	+	+
– solving customer problems	+	+	0	0
– offering systems solutions	+	0	0	-
– effective deployment of sales personnel	0	0	0	0
– effective advertising	0	0	+	+
– construction of image	+	+	+	+
– effective distribution of goods	0	0	+	+
– opening of new channels of distribution	0	0	+	-
– distribution at favourable cost	-	-	-	0
– effective production	0	0	0	+
– employment of new methods of production	0	-	+	0
– production at favourable cost	-	0	-	+
– development of new products	0	+	0	+
– obtaining sources of finance	-	0	+	+
– employment of highly-qualified workforce	0	+	+	+
– interdisciplinary cooperation	+	+	+	+
– employment of well-tested management systems	0	+	+	+
– employment of highly-qualified key workers	+	+	+	+
– provision of well-founded information	-	0	+	+
– the realisation of plans of cooperation, participation and acquisition	-	+	+	+

Present State	+	relevant capability very highly developed
	0	relevant capability at medium stage of development
	-	relevant capability at low stage of development
Assessment of Future	+	relevant capability very important
	0	relevant capability important
	-	relevant capability of lesser importance

[43] Taken from: Pümpin, C., Management strategischer Erfolgspositionen, Berne and Stuttgart 1982, pp. 152–153.

When considering the product-related capabilities of German companies on the world market, the capacity for individual problem-solving is worthy of particular mention. In this case products are not produced in series, but are produced individually, using certain modules, for a specific foreign customer. The individual transaction has become the dominant foreign trade model for many German companies. This is particularly true of the large plant construction sector.[44] The combination of mature technology with individual customer attention has become the fundamental strategic success position for many German companies.

Functional capabilities in the International Marketing of German companies are characterised by the outstanding readiness of these companies to provide, in addition to basic performance, a comprehensive range of back-up services oriented towards foreign trade, such as financial assistance, training assistance or construction, repair or service back-up.

Moreover, within the spectrum of market-related capabilities, it is personal communication to which German companies assign crucial importance for International Marketing.[45] Through personal contact there are demolished those legal, linguistic and above all cultural inhibitions which contribute to psychological distance in International Marketing. The analysis of strategic success positions thus represents an important precondition for the strategic planning of the international activities of a company.

8. Analysis of Market Entry Alternatives

An important instrument of Strategic International Marketing is the analysis and choice of market entry alternatives. Perlitz[46] has developed a specific **pattern analysis** for this. Within the framework of this pattern analysis there takes place an evaluation of the possible international market entry strategies, with reference to certain qualitative features. The major alternatives are:

- exports
- direct investment (with different grades of participation) and
- franchises/licences

[44] Cf. Backhaus, K., Investitionsgüter-Marketing, Munich 1982, pp. 95 ff.

[45] Cf. Meissner, H. G., Außenhandels-Marketing, Stuttgart 1981, p. 78.

[46] Cf. Perlitz, M., Absatzorientierte Internationalisierungsstrategien, unpublished diss., Bochun 1979; cf. Backhaus, K., Investitionsgüter-Marketing, Munich 1982, p. 155.

Table 30. Pattern analysis[47]

Qualitative goals / Strategies	Possibility of opening up the market (Z1)	politically safe markets (Z2)	securing of raw materials (Z3)	low financial burden (Z4)	avoidance of labour disputes (Z5)	figure of relevance (R)
Weighting	0.20	0.10	0.15	0.30	0.25	
Export alternative (A1)	0.20	0.30	0.00	0.15	0.80	0.3150
Direct investment alternative (A2)	0.70	0.60	1.00	0.05	0.05	0.3775
Licensing alternative (A3)	0.10	0.10	0.00	0.80	0.15	0.3075

The possible alternatives for opening up the market are evaluated with respect to the various targets (21) to (25) with values assigned between 0 and 1. If the values of the individual targets are weighted and multiplied with the values and then added, one obtains the figure of relevance for each alternative. In the example given of pattern analysis the alternative A2 represents the most favourable possibility (Table 30).

The market entry alternatives arise in the context of the strategic decision problem as a resultant between the attractiveness of an international market and the specific difficulties connected with entering it. Simon[48] has undertaken a simultaneous evaluation of attractiveness and entry difficulty for 10 selected markets (Diagram 33).

Under the heading of strategic aspects it is important for companies to be aware of specific barriers to entry and and to evaluate them. The attractiveness of a market does not of itself form a sufficient basis for judging the opportunities which foreign activities may offer. This must be judged with respect to the entry barriers present in each case. Japan provides a classic example of the presence of market entry barriers which are partly the result of political decisions of the Japanese government, but are to a greater extent the result of the socio-cultural structure of the country. Once the specific barriers to market entry have been studied for each case, it is then possible to weight the

[47] Taken from: Backhaus, K., Investitionsgüter-Marketing, Munich 1982, p. 155.
[48] Cf. Simon, H., Eintrittsbarrieren und Eintrittsstrategien im japanischen Markt, in: ZfbF, Vol. 37, No. 11 (Nov. 1985), pp. 943–955.

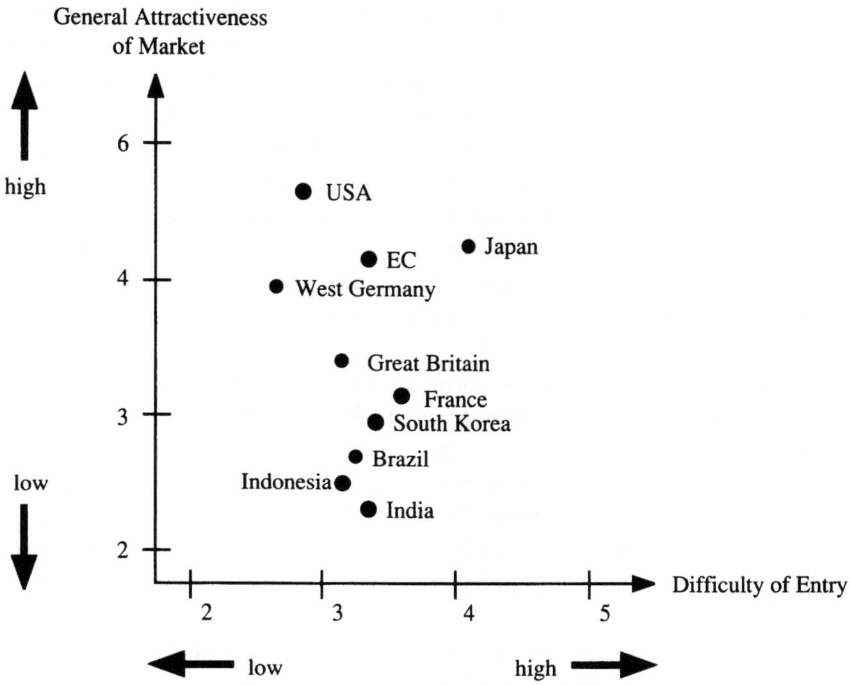

Diagram 33. General market attractiveness and difficulty of entry for 10 selected markets[49]

individual marketing instruments for the relevant foreign market, a process which is once more particularly clear if one compares Germany and Japan.[50]

9. Planning Processes in Strategic International Marketing

The concepts and the methods of Strategic International Marketing must be incorparated into the general planning processes of companies. The result of these efforts is international strategic planning, a combination of strategic planning and international planning. Owing to the uncertainty of long-term developments strategic planning presents special difficulties, and Internatio-

[49] Taken from: Simon, H., Eintrittsbarrieren und Eintrittsstrategien im japanischen Markt, in: ZfbF, Vol. 37, No. 11 (Nov. 1985), p. 944.
[50] Cf. Meissner, H. G., Japanische und deutsche Marketingstrategien: Ein struktureller Vergleich, in: Mitteilungen der Bundesstelle für Außenhandelsinformation, November 1985.

nal Marketing is characterised by specific problem fields, which have their origins especially in the range of differences in the markets which confront international planning. Strategic international planning therefore makes especially high demands on the planning departments of companies.

One encounters the view, expressed emphatically by companies and in academic literature, that is both necessary and appropriate to construct strategic planning on a double foundation. One must distinguish here between the two opposed , but complementary, strategic tendencies of basic planning in the form of **top-down planning**, which is carried out by management, and **bottom-up planning**, planning which is area-specific and based on division into various strategic business units. The interaction of top-down planning and bottom-up planning results in the formulation of goals and strategies, but also in the decisions on budgeting, which is what determines the action and market behaviour of companies. These budgeting decisions concerning e.g investment and advertising budgets can then be compared with the effective results after the planning period and thereby checked and, if necessary, adjusted.

In the area of International Marketing the tendency towards decentralised planning has managed to establish itself. Thus, for example, the Schott Glassworks in Mainz has over 40 production plants in 30 countries and futhermore over 300 subsidiaries in 100 different countries. The foreign quota(exports and turnover of the foreign affiliates) amounts to 63% of the world turnover of the Schott Group [51]. One may see from this world-wide dispersal of market activities that they may no longer be solely or even predominantly planned in all details from Mainz. The role of the headquarters can now only consist in coordinating the planning activities of the individual affiliates and subsidiaries, and it must restrict itself to formulating the global marketing goals and strategies of the group of companies. It is therefore necessary to combine central with decentralised strategic planning, and for this the system of information and reports in the companies must be built up and expanded in an appropriate manner. Diagram 34 illustrates how top-down planning and bottom-up planning work together.

In the large international companies the determination of international planning also takes place at an intermediate divisional level, and here the divisional form of organisation can be oriented either towards regional or towards product-specific aspects. The process of stategy formulation in an international or multinational company then takes place according to the pattern in Diagram 35.

---

[51] Cf. Klein, H. J., Stationen zum Erfolg im größten Spezialglasmarkt der Welt, Lecture at the 39th Conference of German Business Scientists on the 15th Oct. 1985 in Berlin.

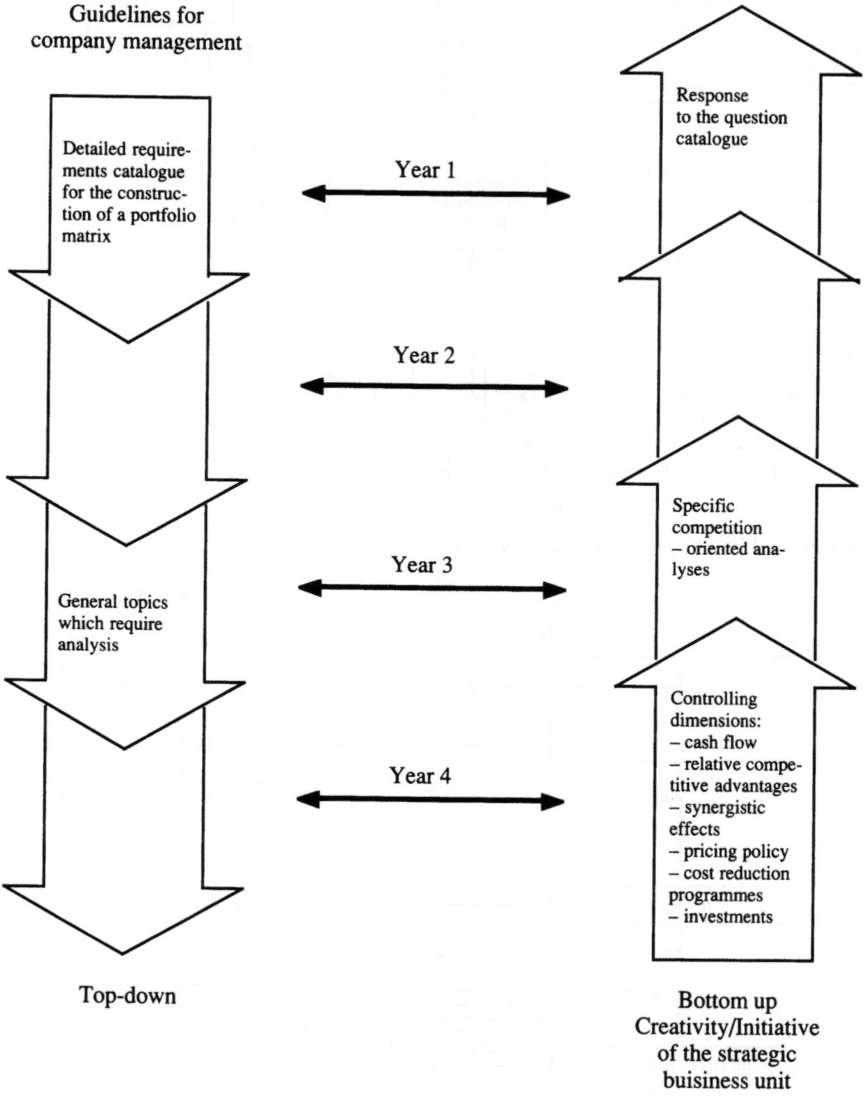

Diagram 34. The interaction of top-down and bottom-up planning[52]

[52] Cf. Hinterhuber, H. H., Strategische Unternehmungsführung, 3rd Edn., Berlin and New York 1984, p. 167.

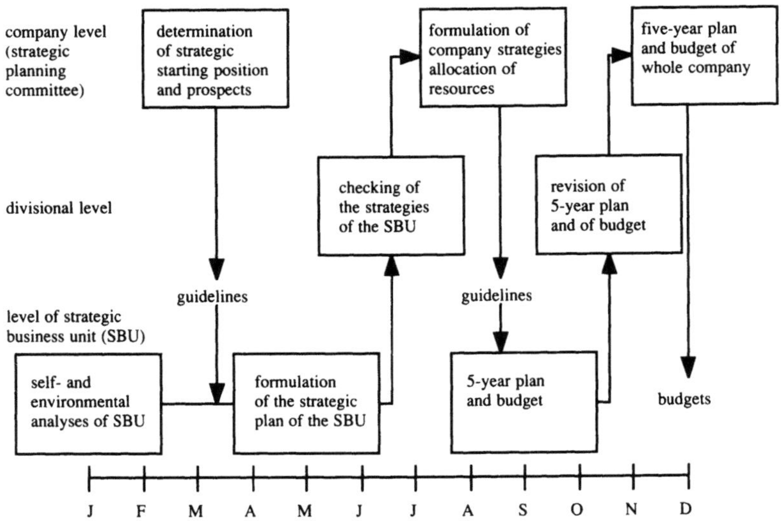

Diagram 35. The process of strategy formulation[53]

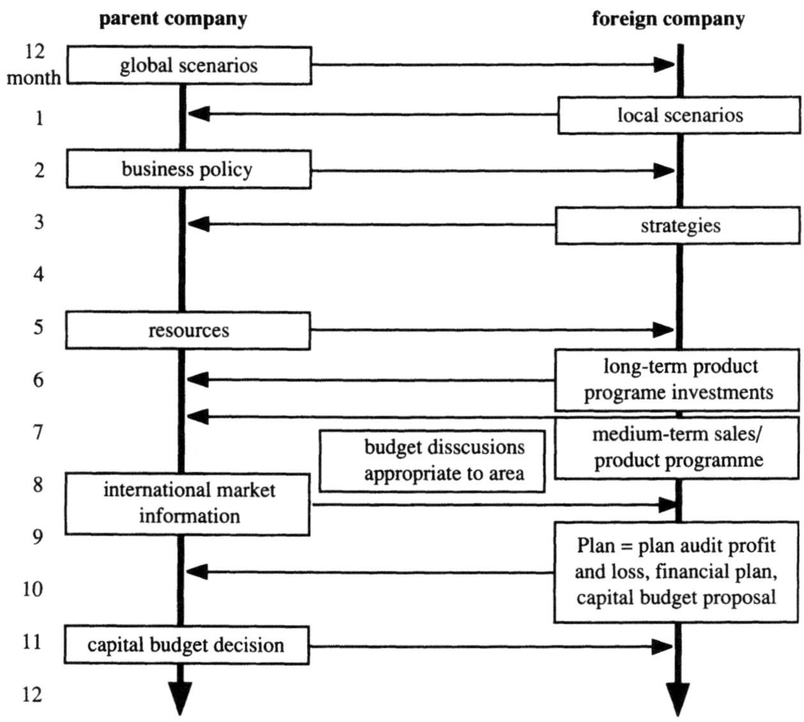

Diagram 36. The vertical matching of international plans[54]

[53] Taken from: Hinterhuber, H. H., Strategische Unternehmungsführung, 3rd Edn., New York 1984, p. 166.
[54] Taken from: Arbeitskreis "Organisation international tätiger Unternehmen" der Schmalenbachgesellschaft, Organisation des Planungsprozesses in international tätigen Unternehmen, in: ZfBF, Vol 31, 1979, p. 31.

The vertical matching of plan between parent company and the individual national or regional strategic business units then comes into being according to Diagram 36.

On the basis of company targets, the conditions prevailing in the international environment and the analysis of possible alternative strategies, it is necessary to set up a **strategic plan**[55], which sets out in differentiated form various competencies in planning and in decision which are proper to the company headquaters and to the affiliates or strategic business units (Table 31).

Table 31. The involvement of international management in strategic planning[56]

	Company Headquarters		Affiliate	
	Top Management	Section Heads	General Management	Section Heads
Analysis of the initial situation	Layout of planning periods and methodology	Layout of informational content and formal framework	Supervision of implementation, summary	Implementation
Interpretation	Transmission of the experience of other countries	Approval	Correction and approval of the interpretation	Implementation
Target-setting	Layout of overall company targets, approval of the targets	Layout of company targets	Layout of production targets	Targets in the executive sections
Strategy development	Layout of fundamental strategy, e.g. growth strategy	Transmission of the experience of other countries, advice	Adjustment and structuring, summary	Suggestion of alternatives

[55] Cf. Majaro, S., International Marketing, London 1977, pp. 189 ff.

[56] Taken from: Höfner, K., Eggle, R., Internationales Management, in: Rationalisierung, Vol. 33 (1982), No. 7/8, p. 150.

	Company Headquarters		Affiliate	
	Top Management	Section Heads	General Management	Section Heads
Strategy evaluation	Summary, approval	Checking for synergistic effects	Checking for financial consequences and feasibility	Checking for financial consequences
Strategy optimization	Approval of overall planning	Transmission of experiences, summary	Coordination of optimization measures, summary	Evaluation of suggestions
Realisation	Continuous observation	Sectional plans of whole company	Overall plans of affiliates	Sectional plans of affiliates
Checks and controls	Overall planning and sectional planning	Overall plans of affiliates	Sectional plans	Plans for corrective measures

The formal planning system for the individual international strategic business units arises as follows:

1 Business development in the past and projection onto the planning horizon,
2 Analysis of previous development and prognosis for the planning period,
3 Success factors in the competition,
4 Analysis of strengths and weaknesses,
5 Measures for attaining the strategic goals,
6 Necessary expenditure (budgets), spread over the planning period.

Strategic planning in an international company requires a very high level of effort in the fields of information and decision-making. This cannot be adequately dealt with by written communication alone but must also be supported by intense personal communication. Indeed this work is frequently carried out in planning workshops in the company headquarters,which are attended by the colleagues concerned from the individual country- and product-specific strategie business units. The task of these planning workshops is to provide a strategic plan both for the individual strategic business units and for the whole company.[57]

A precondition of this is that the companies have available to them a conceptual overall model which they may use to comprehend systematically and to correlate in a meaningful way all the individual factors of the international environment, of technological development and of sociocultural change with respect to the strengths and weaknesses of a company and of its important competitors.[58]

It is precisely through strategic planning that learning curves regularly arise in firms, which lead to colleagues and management gaining increased insight into International Marketing developments and relationships. They obtain new understanding and new knowledge, and this can lead to adjustments and alterations in their planning. Such learning curves are consciously triggered in the context of strategic planning. They represent an important instrument of flexible and creative adjustment to the dynamic of the international marketplace.[59]

---

[57] Cf. Aaker, D. A., Strategic Market Management, New York, 1984, p. 302.

[58] Cf. Sheth, J. N., A Conceptual Model of Long-Range Multinational Marketing, in: Jain, S.C., Tucker, L. jr., (Eds.), International Marketing: Managerial Perspectives, Boston/Mass. 1979, pp. 424–432.

[59] Cf. Ansoff, H.I., Declerck, R.P., Hayes, R.L., From Strategic Planning to Strategic Management, in: Hahn, D., Taylor, B. (Eds.), Strategische Unternehmungsplanung, 3rd Edn. Würzburg, 1984, p. 511.

I. Strategic Global Marketing

1. The Significance of Global Marketing

Strategic International Marketing is gaining in importance for companies under the pressure and the increasing influence now being exerted by global worldwide marketing strategies. Global Marketing means that companies no longer think in national or in regional categories and plan their activities within these, but rather that their concepts now have worldwide dimensions. Global Marketing is leading to an increasing international interlinking of commercial, technological, social and political structures in the world. This interlinking, which expresses itself in the disproportionately large growth in world trade and in the establishment of economic unions along the lines of the European Community, entails considerable changes in the international environment of companies. It has also led to an acceleration of the processes of change and adjustment in the world, and these are particularly evident in the threshold countries. The world economy is therefore also characterised by a high level of discontinuity, and companies find themselves faced with the necessity of coming to terms ever faster and ever more comprehensively with these processes of change – and at times dramatic change – in the world economy.

It was above all the multinational companies who first put the concept of a global company strategy into practice. The growing significance of the multinational companies for the development of the world economy and their increasing commercial and, to some extent too, political power, give rise to additional opportunities, but also to new forms of tension and confrontation; these in their turn act back upon not only the multinational companies, but upon all companies which pursue international activities.[1]

In view of the complexity of the factors of influence and of the consequences of the decisions taken by companies, Global Marketing cannot be carried out on an ad hoc or random basis, but is as a matter of necessity always bound

[1] Cf. Vernon, R., Future of the Multinational Enterprise, in: Kindelberger, C. P. (Ed.), The International Corporation, Cambridge/Mass., London 1970, p. 373.

up with strategic planning. The demands made upon the strategic decisions of internationally active companies are further increased by the orientation towards Global Marketing, so that there arises a specifically new dimension of International Marketing:

Strategic Global Marketing

The future of many companies will depend on their abilitiy to make effective use of the opportunities presented by Global Marketing. For many companies this will require new and revised formulations of the overall company targets and of their company philosophy. The essence of the matter will be for companies to become aware of the unity of the world market and to work with it, and to do justice to the differentiation of the national sub-markets.

The development towards Global Marketing is no longer just a matter for the multinational companies; it is rather becoming increasingly important and interesting for even medium-sized companies to pursue a Global Marketing concept. This holds true for a large number of German engineering companies, but it has also come to apply to companies in, say, the food sector.

In view of stagnating and even shrinking national markets and against a background of increasing international competition, the profitability, growth opportunities and order-books of many companies will no longer be catered for within the restrictions of national borders. These will only have a future through a systematic turning towards the market opportunities available internationally. Global Marketing, with its claims to world-wide orientation, adaptability and creativity thus has its effect on the culture of companies. It is thus Global Marketing which will introduce a far-reaching process of change in all areas of activity and on all levels of decision-making in companies. The faster and the more intensively companies adjust to this process of change, the greater their chances will be of using the opportunities provided by Global Marketing for realising their company goals.

In Strategic Global Marketing, political developments in the world assume particular importance for the decisions of companies. With every marketing decision they make, companies also make, indirectly, a political decision. This is, all at once, a matter of the levels of economic development and employment in individual countries, of international debt and rates of exchange, of the political prestige of individual countries and also of the political fate of individual members of their leaderships. Companies are thus becoming much more closely bound to world-political developments than was ever the case previously. At the same time the global decision policies of companies are being politicised, without traditional business management theory being able to offer any companies affected any patterns or models to aid their decisions.

The politicisation of the worldwide commercial activities of the international companies expresses itself in two ways; on the one hand the companies must recognise and also respect the national states and their norms, but at the same time their worldwide involvement relativises the significance of the national states for them. This situation gives rise to a potential field of conflict both for the international companies and for the national states.[2]

Worldwide economic development has led to the growth of an ambivalent attitude towards multinational companies in national states, and particularly among the developing and threshold countries. The national states have a very deep interest in seeing multinational companies become active in their countries as a means to meeting their requirements for technology transfer, economic growth, international market opportunities and new jobs. Many national states also see the growth in prestige and opportunities for exerting political influence which the presence of a number of significant world companies brings to a country. On the other hand the national states wish to keep a check on the multinational companies and also to influence them to some extent in matters of company policy, e.g. with respect to "local content".

This ambivalance gives rise to a new and subtle form of political risk. Political risk exists for internationally active companies no longer solely in the form of acts of war or of armed insurrection, but also and above all in those forms of political risk which are attendant upon party political developments and splits, the formulation of ideological positions and a politicised form of personal and family connections between ruling families and groups and the international companies. These forms of subtle political risk have in the meantime became a problem for Global Marketing throughout the world.

2. Global Marketing Strategies

Global Marketing is to be defined as a company philosophy which systematically orients all decisions and activities of a company towards the requirements and opportunities of the world market. In particular, Global Marketing leads to the explicit design of world-wide strategies of market selection and market operation.

The decision alternatives which present themselves to Global Marketing decision-makers do so within a continuum of the integrated and non-integrated production and market activities of international companies, so that the following four-field matrix arises (Diagram 37).

---

[2] Cf. Brauchlin, E., Wuffli, P. A., Transnationale Unternehmungen und nationale Interessen als unternehmungspolitisches Problem, in: Lück, W., Trommsdorff, V. (Eds.), Internationalisierung der Unternehmung als Problem der Betriebswirtschaftslehre, Berlin 1982, p. 269.

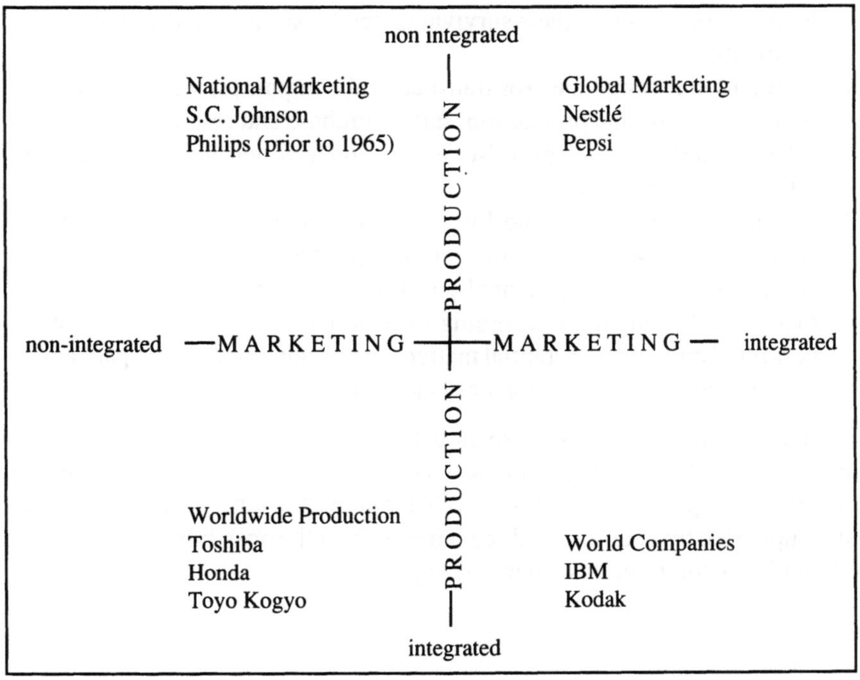

Diagram 37. Global Marketing model[3]

Development here moves from the non-integrated or only weakly integrated strategies to the highly integrated ones , and both in the areas of production and of marketing.

The development into global companies characteristically takes place according to the following pattern :

1) national companies, which produce exclusively for the home market,
2) national companies which carry on export and import business using specialised trading firms (indirect foreign trade)
3) national companies which have their own distribution subsidiaries abroad or with foreign representation (direct foreign trade)
4) national companies with affiliates and subsidiaries abroad for dealing with purchases and for opening up sales markets,
5) international companies, whose export turnover when taken together with the turnover of foreign affiliates and partnerships exceeds turnover on the

[3] Diagram based on: Keegan, W. J., MacMaster, N., Global Strategic Marketing, in: Kirpalani, V.H. (Ed.) International Marketing, Chicago 1983, p. 101.

home market, so that their survival depends on the international market segments,

6) multinational companies (or transnational companies) with a concentration on international production, sales, purchase and research activities in selected markets which promise success and in which environmental conditions are favourable,
7) global companies which no longer pursue a country oriented company strategy, but a worldwide concept. The production programme of these companies is directed principally towards the opportunities of the world market. Differentiation according to regional or national sub-markets is permitted only in insubstantial matters, e.g. in advertising or in packaging. The strategy of these companies is global.

The marketing strategies of these global companies depends on the development of Global Marketing options.[4] The analysis of global scenarios and of their own competitive positions leads to strategic "visions", which are in then turn supported by goal-directed scenarios, so that the possibilities of planning Global Marketing options emerge (Diagram 38).

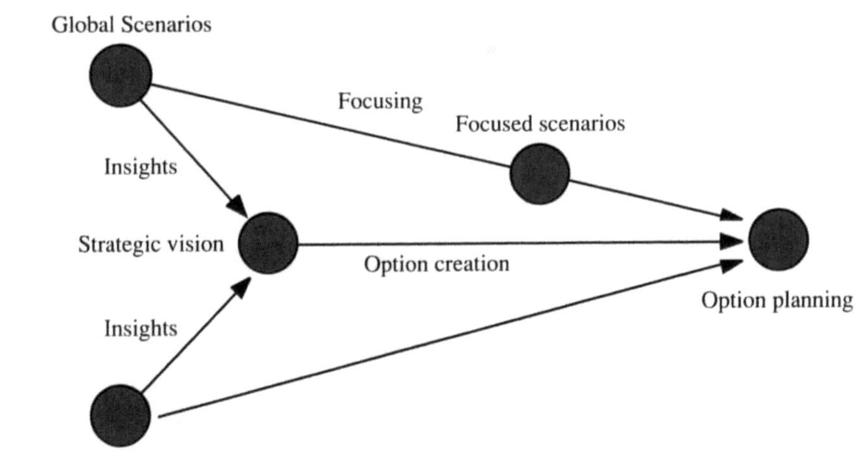

Diagram 38. Strategies in Strategic Global Marketing[5]

[4] Cf. Levitt, T., The Globalization of Markets, in: Havard Business Review, Vol. 61, No. 3 (May 1983), pp. 92–102.
[5] Taken from: Wack, P., Scenarios: Shooting the Rapids, in: Harvard Business Review, Vol. 63, No.6 (Nov./Dec. 1985) p. 150.

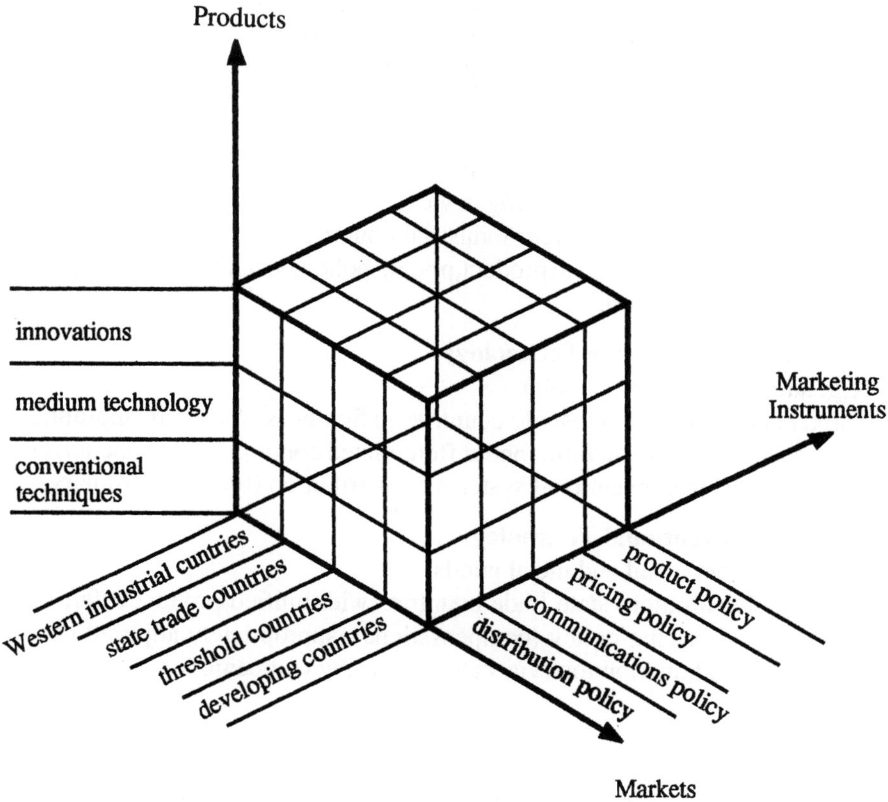

Diagram 39. Decision fields of Global Marketing

Within the framework of global strategic options, the central decision to be made is whether the opening of the market and subsequent market operations are to take place in **standardised or in differentiated form.**

Typically, a decision for Global Marketing entails a tendency towards standardised strategies. The reasons for this may be sought, on the one hand, in the multitude of the regional sub-markets served, which can only be treated in an exceptionally differentiated manner if great expenditure is involved, and on the other hand in the worldwide standardisation in the demands, expectations and behaviour of the consumers.

The question as to standardisation or differentiation[6] cannot be given any universal answer, but must always be addressed to the products or services, to

[6] See especially on this point: Meffert, H., Althans, J., Internationales Marketing, Stuttgart 1982, pp. 98 ff and Kulhavy, E., Internationales Marketing, Linz 1981, pp. 118 ff.

the markets, and finally also to the various marketing functions. This gives rise to a three-dimensional decision field (Diagram 39).

Within the framework of these decision fields various key strategies for Global Marketing may be developed, for example

Type A: Technological Innovation
(e.g. an opto-electronic measuring device)
Market concentration: Western industrial countries with unified marketing strategies, e.g. with respect to product,pricing policy,design of advertising and channels of distribution;

Type B: Medium-range Technology
(e.g. automated machine tools)
Market concentration: threshold countries in Southeast Asia with appropriately adjusted product qualities and differentiated communication and advertising, and using conventional systems of distribution (foreign subsidiary);

Type C: Conventional Technology
(e.g. iron, sheet metal and metal goods)
Market concentration: state trade countries with unified product offer, but differentiated pricing policy (compensations), appropriately adjusted communication and distribution (via state purchasing companies).

If one also additionally considers the possibility of marketing products only nationally, then four types may be described in the decision field between unification and differentiation (Diagram 40).

In addition to these types there exists, in the actual practice of foreign trade, a series of other possible combinations. For Global Marketing it is essential that any specific strategy be undertaken within the framework of the key stategies already laid down in order to preserve uniformity while at the same time maintaining the ability to react flexibly to the requirements of the markets.

The basic decision as to standardisation or differentiation is not made solely in view of the technology on offer, but also with respect to the extent of the psychological distance which a national, international or global company perceives as existing between itself and a foreign market.

Psychological distance has become an important criterion in deciding between international or Global Marketing strategies.[7] Under the heading of psychological distance one measures the extent of the alienness which exists between various countries owing to their different cultures and languages. The

---

[7] Cf. Hallen, L., Wiedersheim-Paul, F., Psychic Distance in International Marketing, Uppsala 1981 (Working Paper).

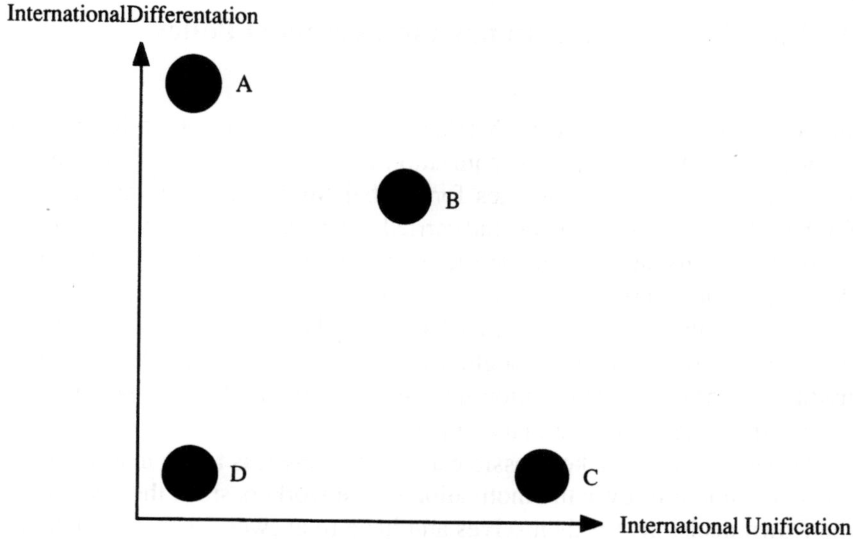

A = higly differentiated products
B = appropriately adjusted products (modulation)
C = worldwide unified products
D = national products

Diagram 40. Types of strategy in the decision field between unification and differentiation

psychological distance between West Germany and Switzerland is slight, but very great between West Germany and Japan. Psychological distance can be ascertained and measured by means of questionnaires. Normally, slight psychological distance leads to intensive processes of international exchange, whereas great psychological distance either complicates international exchange or blocks it completely.

Global Marketing arose after psychological distances in the world had decreased owing to the improved and intensified processes of information and communication. This is an important explanatory factor for the growth of world business and world trade, which points clearly beyond explanations previously pursued, such as e.g. price advantages,technological differences or availability. For this reason it is precisely in Global Marketing that the human bases of marketing decisions become clear. Global Marketing is first and foremost humanistic marketing, and not just technological marketing, political marketing or company-strategic marketing.

3. Aspects of Organisational and Personnel Policy

In the case of Global Strategic Marketing, too, the organisation follows the strategy. A suitably adapted organisation and the corresponding personnel policy are essential prerequisites for Global Marketing. The strategies of Global Marketing are designed and carried out by persons who work together in specific organisations. The long-term success of global strategies therefore depends not least upon organisation and personnel development.[8]

The globalisation of marketing has strengthened the tendency towards decentralised organisation throughout companies worldwide.[9] Owing to their traditional forms of organisation the Japanese trading houses have not yet followed this development in a comparable manner.[10]

Decentralisation makes possible a greater closeness to the market and at the same time improves the motivation of the workers since they can make their own decisions for themselves and have to answer for them. Since the dominant motive for the internationalisation and, increasingly, for the globalisation of companies is to be found in the safeguarding and the opening-up of markets[11], the organisation of companies must be designed in a manner which is especially close to and proper to the the market. In spite of all globalisation, those who work for worldwide companies have not lost their national character and remain bound to their respective national cultures. The decisions of companies which are active throughout the world must therefore be made against the background of the existing national markets and of the available local workforce. This conflict marks current discussion concerning the appropriate and suitable form of organisation. In this context the parent-child relationships of the international companies have a central role to play.[12] The dilemma posed by necessary centralisation versus possible decentralisation dominates the organisational decision processes of companies which are active world-wide.

---

[8] Cf. Leontiades, J., Multinational Corporate Strategy, Lexington/Mass., Toronto 1985, pp. 185 ff.

[9] Cf. Cateora, P. R., International Marketing, 5th. Edn., Homewood/Ill. 1983, pp. 185 ff.

[10] Cf. Kreikebaum, H., Personal- und kommunikationspolitische Aspekte der Unternehmensführung in Japan, in: Dülfer, E. (Ed.), Personelle Aspekte im Internationalen Management, Berlin 1983, pp. 129–157.

[11] Cf. Jahrreiß, W., Zur Theorie der Direktinvestinvestitionen im Ausland, Berlin 1984, pp. 278 ff.

[12] Cf. Welge, M., Management in deutschen multinationalen Unternehmungen, Stuttgart 1980, pp. 222 ff.

Furthermore, the problems of filling management positions in foreign affiliates or partnerships are being discussed very intensively.[13] Global management requires a specific personnel adjustment. In particular, one must distinguish between centrally appointed and locally recruited managers and specialists. In addition so-called **expatriates** play a leading role in filling leading positions in international companies.[14]

It is these expatriates, with their low level of national connections, being as they are no longer closely bound to national and cultural patterns of behaviour, who correspond most closely to the ideal expectations of global companies. They develop an international mangement culture, similar to that found amoung academics, where national connections are more quickly and more throughly relativised, not least as a result of intensive international communication.

Table 32. Strategies for filling foreign business management positions[15]

	ethnocentric	polycentric	geocentric
characteristics of company policy	uniform	differentiated	uniform
	dominated by parent company	oriented towards host country	significance of difference in environment less marked
	international	multinational	global
filling of management positions with	personnel from parent company	locals	management appointed without regard to nationality or origin
quota sent out	medium	zero	high

[13] Cf. Arbeitskreis Karenberg/Meissner der Schmalenbach-Gesellschaft, Auslandsaktivitäten deutscher Unternehmen, Chancen der Zukunftssicherung, Cologne, (Bundesstelle für Außenhandelsinformation) 1983, pp. 52 ff.

[14] Cf. Zeira, Y., Banai, M., Selection of Expatriate Managers in MNCs: The Host-Environment Point of View, in: International Studies of Man & Organisation, Vol. XV, No. 1/1985, pp. 33–51.

[15] Taken from: Pausenberger, E., Die Besetzung von Geschäftsführerpositionen in ausländischen Tochtergesellschaften, in: Dülfer, E. (Ed.), Personelle Aspekte im Internationalen Management, Berlin 1983, p. 55.

Joint ventures make special demands on the co-operation between centrally appointed and locally recruited management personnel. The common company goal which has led to the foundation of the joint ventures must be pursued by managers with differring cultural,political, and educational backgrounds. The manager sent abroad will normally develop a greater sense of loyalty towards the foreign parent company, whereas the local managers will represent more strongly the interests of the local partner. This situation is frequently fraught with the risk of conflict, so that a particularly careful and sensitive personnel policy must be adopted for the management of joint ventures.

Basically, three strategies may be distinguished in the filling of management positions in foreign companies and these may be called the ethnocentric, the polycentric and the geocentric. These company-political concepts represent the basis for alternative appointment strategies (Table 32).

For the realisation and the long-term expansion of their international options, companies must therefore follow a personnel policy which is both conscious in its planning and specific in its tasks. This personnel policy may be sub-divided into three different areas of activity:[16]

- personnel recruitment
- personnel planning and deployment
- training programmes.

When recruiting personnel for international business German companies are finding it increasingly difficult to find suitable workers who are prepared to undertake long-term overseas duties, particulary when these are to take place in countries and places which are not attractive for either climatic, political or cultural reasons. The career of the spouse, the school problems of the children, and fears concerning opportunities in the parent company all contribute to the intensification of this problem of adequate personnel recruitment.

These problems also affect personnel planning for international business and the scope for assigning duties to individual workers, whether male or female. North American and Japanese companies have up to now had fewer problems in this area. In these cases, a longish spell of activity with a foreign company counts as an essential requirement for a career in the organisations concerned.

International personnel planning is primarily concerned with the long-term provision of qualified and motivated personnel for specific foreign postings, in order to avoid short-term ad hoc decisions on personnel policy which can arise in response to immediate needs. To this sphere also belong the

[16] Cf. Cisek, G., Internationale Personalorganisation, Berlin 1974, p. 32.

planning for rotation within the various overseas companies and concrete proposals for reintegration into the parent company subsequent to foreign activity.

In the area of personnel planning companies find themselves confronted with problems which are also typical for the diplomatic services. The rhythm of rotation in international companies is however slower than is normally the case with diplomats. Companies must plan over a longer period and they require time in order to build up a functioning foreign operation. Market knowledge and contacts with the important decision makers of a foreign market require continuity and stability.

In proportion to the duration of a foreign posting, most persons develop an inner sympathy with their host country and thereby a relative alienation from their home country. But there can also arise a hardening of prejudices, which leads to isolation in the country concerned. In the course of time there frequently occurs a displacement of interests and loyalties from the home country to the host country. This process can be partially neutralised by conferences, visits of the company management to the host country and involvement of the overseas managers in the decision processes of the parent company.

A futher significant aspect of organisation and personnel policy for Global Marketing consists in the process of training, and this applies at all levels of the firm (Table 33).

Table 33. Training system for Global Marketing (x=special emphasis in training)

Function \ Area of Training	Environment and Culture	Company Targets	Decision Regulations and Organisation	Technical Requirements
1. Managers sent out	X	X		
2. Local Managers		X	X	
3. Technical Specialists sent out	X		X	X
4. Local Technical Specialists		X	X	

Training should take place on the spot abroad, as well as in the mother country. The training of management personnel is then more strongly concentrated in the mother country whereas technical specialists should be trained mostly at the actual location. The training offers made by German industry for the next generation of management and other personnel from developing countries represent a major competitive factor in Global Marketing.[17]

The training offers made by certain other countries play a similar role, so that Global Marketing is an area of competition not just of products, prices and financial conditions but also of training.

Training involves in addition a cultural transfer process which also attains a long-term strategic significance. Learned patterns and modes of behaviour mark the attitudes and the behaviour of foreign colleagues, customers and potential market partners much more profoundly than a once-off business transaction. To this extent the training offer is more than just a functional aid for companies, it also represents an element of sociocultural change in the world.

4. Strategies of Global Finance

In International Strategic Marketing, financial strategies play an important and often a decisive role.[18] It is only when companies are in a position to take care of financing, in addition to whatever actual supply or investment services they might offer, that many international deals come into being. This applies especially to deals with the developing countries, the threshold countries and also, partly,the state trade countries.

Companies with world-wide involvement must therefore also pursue a global financing strategy. Here it is a matter of a company either being itself in a position to offer the necessary finance for individual projects, or to arrange such finance; both paths may be considered under the heading of "financial engineering".[19] It is also a matter of devising an international risk management strategy for the variety of financial deals with their different conditions and

---

[17] Cf. Carl-Duisberg Centren (Eds.), Ausbildungsangebote der deutschen Wirtschaft für Entwicklungsländer, Part 1, Cologne 1984.

[18] Cf. Meissner, H. G., Finanzierungskonditionen als Instrumente des Exportmarketing, in: Macharzina, K. (Ed.), Finanz- und bankwirtschaftliche Probleme bei internationaler Unternehmenstätigkeit, Stuttgart 1985, pp. 147–162.

[19] Cf. Fieten, R., Financial Engineering – Komponente des industriellen Großanlagengeschäfts, in: Macharzina, K. (Ed.), Finanz- und bankwirtschaftliche Probleme bei internationaler Unternehmenstäigkeit, Stuttgart 1985, pp. 163–194.

obligations. This risk management is further complicated by changes in the rates of exchange, especially in those areas where such changes are primarily an expression of speculative expectations and not of genuine industrial developments.

Just as in other spheres of activity, so too in the areas of financial policy international companies find themselves by comparison with national compa-

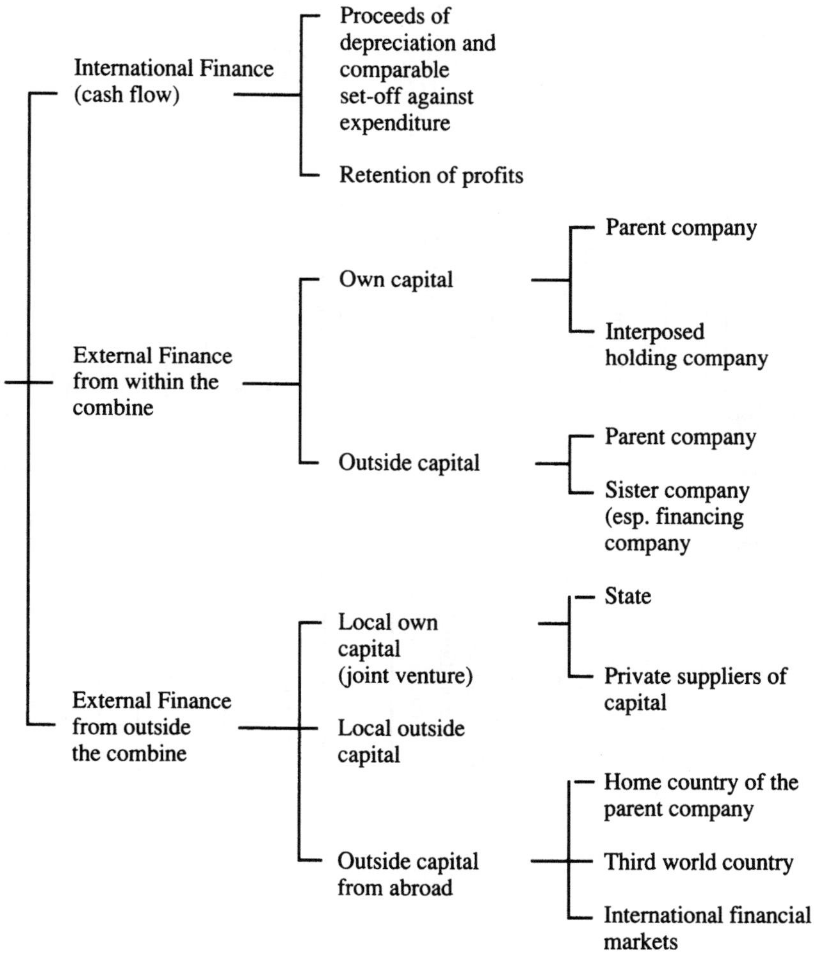

Diagram 41. Possibilities of meeting capital requirements[20]

[20] Pausenberger, E., Finanzpolitik internationaler Unternehmungen: Notwendigkeit und Grenzen der Zentralisierung, in: Wacker, W. H., Haussmann, H., Kumar, B. (Eds.), Internationale Unternehmensführung, Berlin 1981, p. 181.

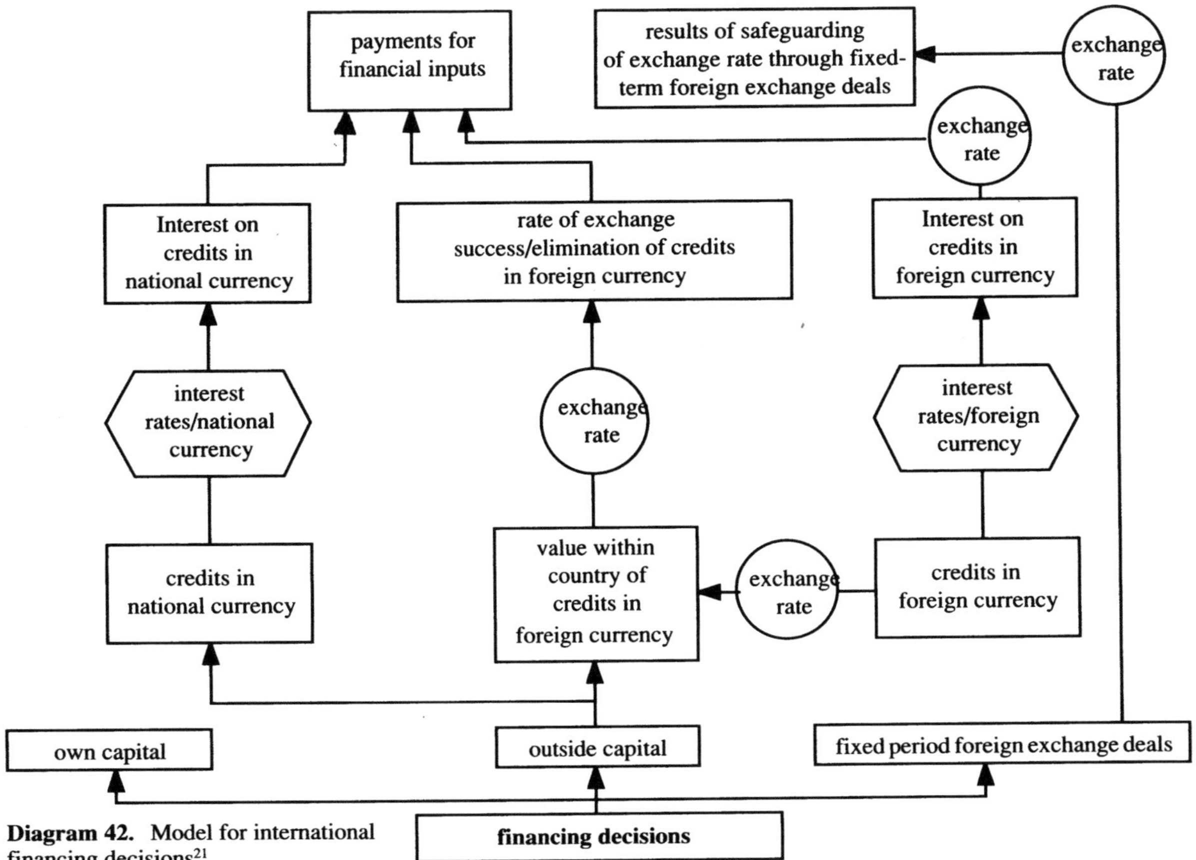

Diagram 42. Model for international financing decisions[21]

[21] Taken from: Dworak, B. M., Das Länderrisiko als bankbetriebliches Problem, Berlin 1985, p. 139.

nies, with a broad spectrum of alternatives to choose from. This holds true for the financial markets, as well as for the institutions, the forms and the conditions of international financing. Pausenberger gives an overview of the possibilities of covering the capital requirements of a foreign affiliate (Diagram 41).

When one is dealing with a variety of foreign affiliates and participations, e.g in the form of joint ventures, the individual involvements add up to an overall international risk. Companies must therefore develop strategies in order to cover this overall financial risk and to make it supportable, without allowing the international involvement to present a risk to the survival of the parent company or of the organisation as a whole.

A model for the financial decisions of international companies was developed by Moser (Diagram 42). This diagram illustrates the complexity of financial decisions and the risk potential linked to them.

When dealing with long-term export credits German companies attempt to cover both the financial risk and the exchange rate risk by presenting invoices made out in West German marks, by revolving hedging deals or by state credit insurances. For export deals with developing countries and state trade countries the existing West German system has proved itself in practice. This system consists of a combination of financing medium- and long-term exports through the Ausfuhrkreditanstalt GmbH (Export Credit Company) with an export credit insurance provided by the Hermes Kreditversicherungs AG. It offers companies a necessary aid for their risk potential, and thus for their assumption of international risks.[22]

For long term supply deals which are not conventionally insured and which are not drawn up within the AKA/Hermes system, the companies themselves remain responsible. The overall risk position of these companies grows in proportion to their international involvement. In order to safeguard themselves in terms of their overall international financial risk, the companies once more adopt portfolio strategies with which they strive to spread the individual risk positions over as many, and as variously structured, countries as possible. Even a concentration of the total risk on an expanding and large market such as the USA does not relieve countries of the exchange rate risk as has been shown for example by German investments in the USA; the rise in the dollar in 1984 and 1985 brought about a situation where these, in terms of German marks, required considerably increased investments, and this had negative consequences for the profitability of the investments.

Also, in matters of foreign investment companies rely, when making their financial decisions, upon state and supranational financial aids, and these are

[22] Cf. Börgers, K.-H., Quambusch, L., Export und Auslandsinvestitionen, Cologne 1985, pp. 60 ff and pp. 80 ff.

provided in West Germany by the Kreditanstalt für Wiederaufbau (Credit Bank for Reconstruction) and the Deutsche Finanzierungsgesellschaft für Beteiligungen in Entwicklungsländren (DEG) (German Bank for Participation in Developing Countries). In addition there are the possibilities of finance offered to those placing orders by the World Bank and its affiliates, and by national and regional banks.[23]

Yet it remains the case with these foreign investments which are promoted and thus made possible with state assistance, that companies still retain their own share of involvement, and on a worldwide basis these involvements once more add up to a global risk position. So once more companies face the necessity of holding this risk within manageable and calculable margins by means of an appropriate portfolio strategy.[24]

The background for these strategies is formed by the expectations concerning the developments of the country risks, particularly with reference to the situation of the international indebtedness of the individual countries.[25] The portfolio strategy, in the context of decisions concerning international financing, is thus closely related to the global risk policy and strategy of international companies.[26]

It is only possible for companies to determine their global risk position when they have available to them an adequate international control system.[27] The construction of an international control system implies the task of drawing up a world balance-sheet, the checking of individual positions on the balance-sheet and the estimation of world success with reference to is-ought comparisons in temporal and functional progression, as well as in currencies such as the German mark.

In international controlling, a decision must be made as to whether the point of reference is to be the home country or the host country. The

---

[23] Cf. Börgers, K.-H., Quambusch, L., Export und Auslandsinvestitionen, Cologne 1985, pp. 131 ff.

[24] Cf. Casey, D., International Investing, New York 1981.

[25] Cf. on this point: Schmidt, R., Analyse der Länderverschuldung aus der Sicht der international tätigen Bank, in: Macharzina, K. (Ed.), Finanz- und betriebswirtschaftliche Probleme bei internationaler Unternehmenstätigkeit, Stuttgart 1985, pp. 47–73 and Meissner, H. G., Singer, H., Jahn, W., Banning, Th. E., Die internationale Verschuldung als Problem der Unternehmensführung, Vol. 237 of the Wissenschaftliche Arbeitsgemeinschaft für Technik und Wirtschaft des Landes Nordrhein-Westfalen, Dortmund 1985.

[26] Cf. Cateora, P. R., International Marketing, 5th. Edn., Homewood/Ill. 1983, pp. 706 ff; Markowitz, H. M., Portfolio Selection, Efficient Diversification of Investments, New York 1959.

[27] Cf. Falkenhausen, F. Freiherr von, Organisation und Kontrolle in multinationalen Unternehmen, in: ZfbF, Vol. 1975, Special Supplement 4, pp. 75–89; Baumann, K.-H., Das Rechnungswesen als Instrument zur Steuerung und Kontrolle von US-Tochtergesellschaften deutscher Unternehmen, in: Zfbf, Vol. 38, No. 5 (May 1969), pp. 425–432; Zünd, A., Kontrolle und Revision in der multinationalen Unternehmung, Berne 1971.

neutralisation of inflationary processes (with their attendant risk of striving after illusory profits) on the various foreign markets is extremely important in international controlling, as is the consideration of variations in the rate of exchange (with the risk of loss or the opportunity of gain dependent on these rates).

5. Global Information and Communications Strategies

Global Marketing requires information and communication which are greater both in extent and in sensitivity than is the case either in national or in limitedly international markets. On the national markets some brands establish themselves and firms can then build upon a comprehensive and general awareness of the brand. In the international market this brand awareness and accompanying firm image, and thus an identity for the company concerned, must all be created. In Global Marketing these requirements are further increased. Socio-cultural differences make it necessary to examine conditions in the individual sub-markets of the world with a much greater degree of sensitivity than is necessary on the national market. In the national market there is to a large extent a common cultural consensus, which does not have to be first discovered or explained.

For the international companies there thus arises the problem of having to come to grips with the particularities of the individual sub-markets of the world. In the context of the increasing decentralisation of international business, this is carried out by the foreign affiliates or by the subsidiaries on the spot. At the same time, however, the global identity of this company must be created and further developed. A company gains such an identity by presenting a uniform image worldwide and by identical approach and behaviour.

The central problem in the area of information and communications strategies for international companies therefore consists in the internal adjustment and synchronisation between the global image which the parent company possesses (or strives after) and the informational and advertising strategies which are pursued by the individual national affiliates or subsidiaries. A harmony must be created between these two fields of endeavour, namely the creation of a global firm image and the advertising strategies of the individual affiliates, if important factors in international success are not to be neglected.

This field of tension between parent company and affiliates of international organisations produces typical discontinuities in information and communications strategies and leads ultimately, owing to structural stresses, to

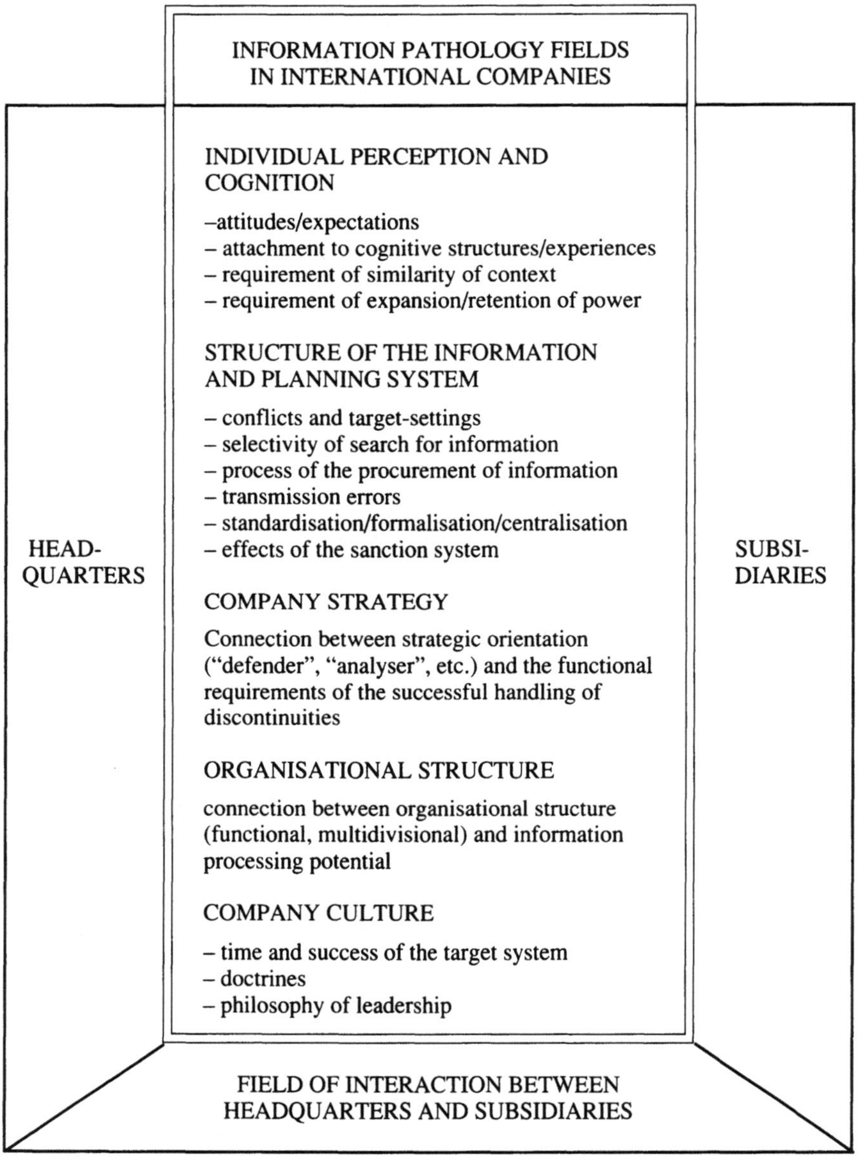

Diagram 43. Reference framework for the systematization of information pathologies in international companies[28]

[28] Taken from: Macharzina, K., Strategische Fehlentscheidungen in der internationalen Unternehmung als Folge von Informationspathologien, in: Macharzina, K. (Ed.), Diskontinuitätenmanagement, Berlin 1984, p. 89.

characteristic informational pathologies. Macharinza has systematised the framework of reference of these informational policies in international companies as shown in Diagram 43.

International marketing communication is carried out within a variety of sociocultural systems. A comparison of successful marketing strategies in West Germany and in Japan shows significant differences between the two countries. An entry onto the Japanese market can only take place with any hope of success if the foreign companies concerned adjust themselves very precisely to the communicative and cultural particularities of the Japanese market.[29]

In actual fact such a differentiation must be carried out with every single foreign market. Even the market of the Netherlands cannot be opened up according to the same pattern and with the same advertising spots as the market of North Rhine-Westphalia. The market of Spain requires a different information and communications strategy from the market of Portugal.

The increasing significance of international (and in many cases this means American) advertising agencies, business consultancies and market research institutes leads to a situation in which it is no longer so much the differences which are noticed, but the common points, and it is these common points which are emphasised. To the extent to which an identical world culture is in the process of formation, such a procedure is indeed sensible and acceptable. But the world is however in a polarised state, a uniform culture is emerging but at the same time national, regional and even local identities are gaining in importance.[30]

Therefore in the context of Global Marketing concepts the parent company, in consultation with its affiliates, must develop an integrated information and communications policy (Diagram 44).

The communication strategies of International Marketing are much more strongly and more clearly personalised than is the case in the national markets. This is connected with the increasing significance of investment goods and large plant construction for the world economy and also with the variations encountered in the legal and foreign trade systems of the various countries. Lasting international relationships come about on the basis of personal contact and trust among people. Persons from differing cultural environments come together in negotiating situations and it is in the interest of all concerned to find

[29] Cf. Meissner, H. G., Japanische und deutsche Marketingstrategien: Ein struktureller Vergleich, in: Mitteilungen der Bundesstelle für Außenhandelsinformation, November 1985.

[30] Cf. Dunn, W. S., Effect of National Identity on Multinational Promotional Strategy in Europe, in: Jain, S. C., Tucker, L. R.jr., (Eds.) International Marketing: Managerial Perspectives, Boston/Mass. 1979, pp. 355–368.

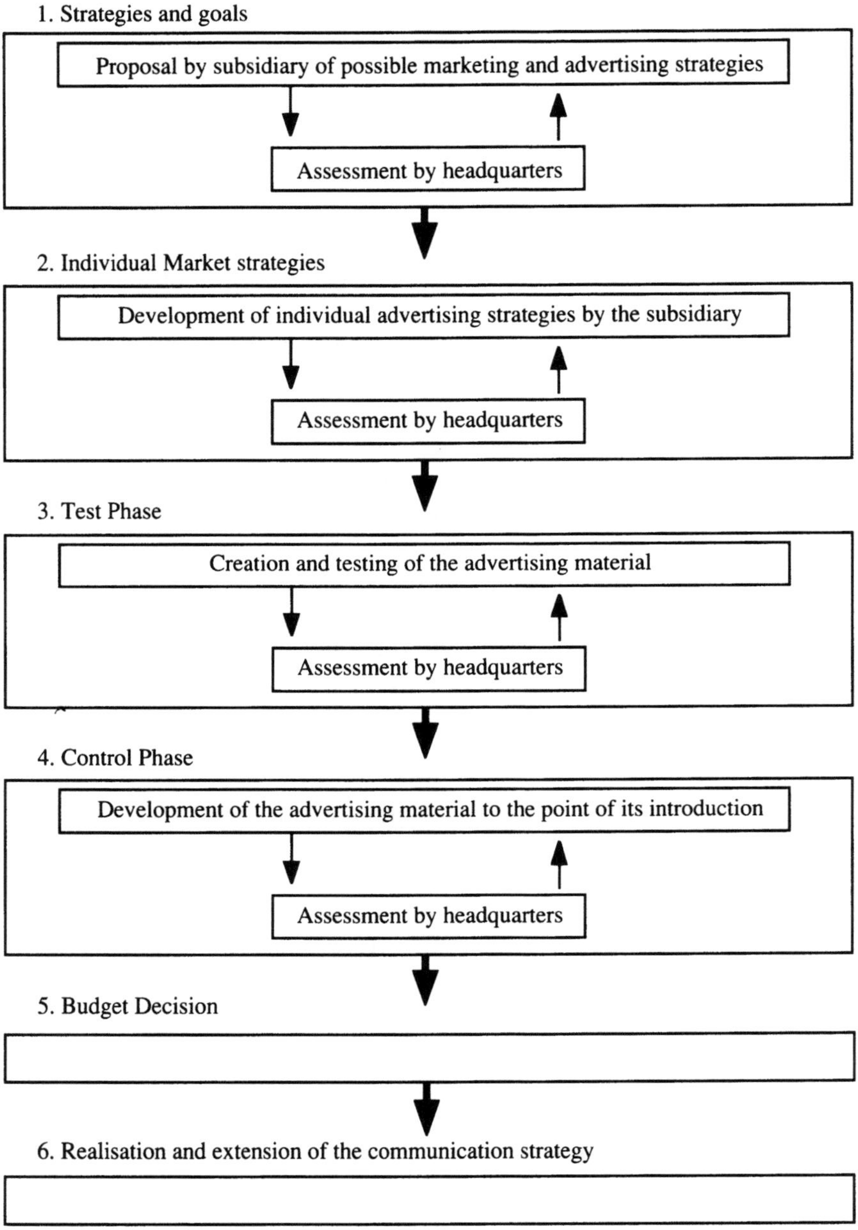

Diagram 44. Decision and development scheme for international communications campaigns[31]

[31] Diagram based on: Peebles, D. M., Ryans, K. jr., Vernon, I. R., Coordinating International Advertising, in: Jain, S. C., Tucker, L. R. jr. (Eds.), International Marketing: Managerial Perspectives, Boston/Mass. 1979, p. 348.

a working business arrangement. The basis for such agreements lies in the extent of the personal trust built up between the partners to the agreement.[32]

Globally oriented companies are always in search of their own identities. The dynamic of the socio-political field in which they operate is so great that they are being constantly sucked into the whirlpool of world-political and world-economic changes, so that positions which were still sensible and promising just a few short years ago have quickly ceased to be so because in the meantime events have intervened and developments have taken place which have led to dramatic alterations of the environment. The special challenge which is presented to international companies therefore consists in the development of an unmistakable identity in the midst of this whirlpool of change. Of necessity this requires great flexibility on the part of the companies and a permanent process of adjustment, but it also requires worldwide efforts in the field of communications.

Such processes of adjustment regularly lead to great unrest in the organisation. The personnel, and often too the leading executives, are content when they have reached a certain plateau in their international activities and they are psychologically not in a position immediately and radically to question familiar paths and results achieved yet again, in order to seek a new plateau. The history of the success of international companies is the history of their ability to adjust and change. If the dynamic is lost or is no longer strong enough, the capacity for international action of these companies suffers, so that they fall back to a lower level of international efficency and once more lose their international identity.

6. Perspectives in the Development of Global Strategic Marketing

The universal connection of the world economy and world politics[33] has always exerted considerable influence on the marketing strategies of companies. The historical impulse towards political understanding and partial cooperation among the countries of the world will also in the future have far-reaching effects on the marketing strategies of international companies. This

[32] Cf. Graham, J. L., Sano, Y., Smart Bargaining – Doing Business with the Japanese, Cambridge/Mass. 1984; Graham, J. L., Campbell, N., Jolibert, A., Meissner, H. G., A Comparision of Marketing Negotiations in France, Germany, the United Kingdom and the United States, Project Report, University of Southern California 1985.

[33] Cf. Elliot, W.Y., Weltwirtschaft und Weltpolitik, Munich 1957.

tendency will be supported and intensified by the improvement and expansion of international communication. It is precisely the activities of the international companies which have led to the world's becoming smaller and more uniform. The ideological confrontation between the western world and the countries of centrally planned economy is degenerating into technical details, although at present these are still powerful and dangerous enough. But the common interests in economic growth, technological development and ecological responsibility for the state of the world are working more strongly towards a process of rapprochement and harmony than towards the development of confrontation and isolation.

It is much more difficult to predict the significance of fundamentalist currents in the Arab world for the future of world politics and the world economy. A disruptive potential has arisen here whose effects are extremely difficult to predict.

On the other hand, the Far East in particular has seen a process of accelerated integration into the world economy, from which especially countries such as Japan and more recently too the Republic of China, the Republic of Korea, Indonesia and, increasingly, India all profit. In these countries international cooperation has led to processes of economic growth which have brought about fundamental readjustment and change in this group of nations. The interest of these countries lies therefore in the reinforcement and possible expansion of the international division of labour.

Global Strategic Marketing has up to now been the domain of the international companies, and in particular of the multinational companies which are active throughout the world. The expansion and the further development of the world economy will increase the significance of Strategic International Marketing for medium-sized companies too. Even today a large number of medium-sized German companies are intensively involved in the international division of labour. This is particularly true of those companies which offer technologicaly mature products of worldwide interest. The transfer of the concepts of Strategic Global Marketing to medium-sized companies will be a process which will require time and which will lead in the long term to an accommodation in the cultures of these companies.

It is beyond doubt that the significance of Strategic International Marketing will play an increasing role in the management decisions of companies. The companies will have to accommodate themselves to this development towards Strategic International Marketing if they are to remain profitable in the worldwide processes of growth and development.

For the scientific field of business management there thereby opens a gateway to a whole new dimension of academic research and theory. Business management theory in West Germany has up to now concerned itself with this process only very incompletely and half-heartedly, although it is above all the large German companies, which have traditionally provided the model for German business management theory ever since the work of Eugen Schmalenbach, which are being drawn more and more strongly into the processes of the international division of labour, as is indicated by the increasing export and import quotas, and also by the increase in direct foreign investments.

German business management theory has considerable ground to make up in the area of International Management. It will be necessary to fill this gap in the years to come in the interest both of companies and of the self-image of a practice-oriented applied science.

List of Diagrams

List of Tables

Bibliography

Aaker, David A., Strategic Market Management, New York, 1984

Abegglen, James C., Stalk, George, Raisha,the Japanese Corporation, New York 1985

Albach, Horst, Strategische Unternehmensplanung bei erhöhter Unsicherheit, in: ZfB, vol. 48, No.8, pp. 702-715

Albach, Horst, Die internationale Unternehmung als Gegenstand betriebswirtschafticher Forschung, in: ZfB, ,51.vol., supplement 1/81, pp.13-24

Ansoff, Igor, Management-Strategie, Munich 1966

Ansoff, H.I., Declerck, R.P., Hayes, R.L., From Strategic Planning to Strategic Management, in: Hahn, Dietger, Taylor, Bernard (Eds.), Strategische Unternehmungsplanung, 3rd Edn. Würzburg, 1984, pp.479-516

Arbeitsgemeinschaft Großanlagenbau in: VDMA, (Eds.), Lagenbericht 1985, Frankfurt/ M.1986

Arbeitskreis Karenberg/Meissner der Schmalenbach-Gesellschaft, Aufbau von Unternehmungen in Entwicklungsländern, Cologne (Bundesstelle für Außenhandelsinformation) 1974

Arbeitskreis Karenberg/Meissner der Schmalenbach-Geselschaft, Auslandsaktivitäten deutscher Unternehmen, Chancen der Zukunftssicherung, Cologne, (Bundesstelle für Außenhandelsinformation) 1983

Backhaus, Klaus, Auftragsplanung im industriellen Anlagengeschäft, Stuttgart 1980

Backhaus, Klaus, Investitionsgüter-Marketing, Munich 1982

Ballon, Robert j. (Eds.), Japan's Market and Foreign Business, Tokyo 1971

Banning, Thomas E., Lebensstilorientierte Marketing-Theorie, Heidelberg 1987

Baumann, Karl-Heinz, Das Rechnungswesen als Instrument zur Steuerung und Kontrolle von US-Tochtergesellschaften deutscher Unternehmen, in: ZfbF, vol. 38, No. 5 (May 1969), pp. 425–432

Berekoven, Ludwig, Internationale Verbrauchsangleichung, Nürnberg 1977

Berekoven, Ludwig, Internationales Marketing, 2.Edn., Herne and Berlin 1985

Bernkopf, Günter, Strategien zur Auswahl ausländischer Märkte, Munich 1980

Bleicher, Knut, Zur organisatorischen Entwicklung multinationaler Unternehmungen, in: Zeitschrift für Organisation, vol. 41 (1972). Nos. 7 and 8, pp. 330-338 und pp. 415-425

Börgers, Karl-Heinz, Quambusch, Liesel, Export und Auslandsinvestitionen, Cologne 1985

BMWi (Eds.), Hochtechnologien und internationale Wettbewerbsfähigkeit der deutschen Wirtschaft, Document No. 263 July 1984

Brauchlin, Emil, Wuffli, Peter, A., Transnationale Unternehmungen und nationale Interessen als unternehmungspolitisches Problem, in: Lück, Wolfgang, Trommsdorff, Volker (Eds.), Internationalisierung der Unternehmung als Problem der Betriebswirtschaftslehre, Berlin 1982, pp. 269-290

Brophy, Sean A. The Strategic Management of Irish Enterprises 1934-1984, Dublin 1985

Bundesstelle für Außenhandelsinformation (BfAi)(Eds.), Informationsbedarf und Informationsverhalten ausgewählter Wirtschaftszweige bezüglich außenwirtschaftlicher Informationen, Cologne 1985

Busse von Colbe, Walter, Müller, Eberhard (Eds.), Planungs- und Kontrollrechnungen in internationalen Konzernen, Sonderheft 17 der ZfbF, Vol.36 1984
Byars, Lloyd L., Strategic Management: Planning and Implementation, Concepts and Cases, New York, e.a. 1984
Carl-Duisberg Centren (Eds.), Ausbildungsangebote der deutschen Wirtschaft für Entwicklungsländer, Cologne 1984
Casey, Douglas, International Investing, New York 1981
Cateora, Philip R., International Marketing, 5th Edn., Homewood/III. 1983
Cisek, Günter, Internationale Personalorganisation, Berlin 1974
Commerzbank, (Eds.), Business Notes of Sept./Oct. 1984
Cramer, Michael, Das internationale Kreditgeschäft der Banken, Wiesbaden 1981
Deutsche Bank (Eds.), Außenwirtschafts-Alphabet, Ratgeber für das Auslandsgeschäft, Frankfurt, continous series
Deutsche Bundesbank, company report 1983
Deutsche Bundesbank (Eds.), Monthly Reports of the German Federal Bank 1985, no. 3
Deutsche Bundesbank (Eds.), Monthly Reports of the German Federal Bank 1989, no. 4
Dichtl , Erwin, Issing, Ottmar (Eds.), Exporte als Herausforderung für die deutsche Wirtschaft, Cologne 1984
Dresdner Bank (Eds.), Wissenswertes für den Exporteur, (continuous series)
Dülfer, Eberhard, Zum Problem der Umweltberücksichtigung im "Internationalen Management", in: Pausenberger, Ehrenfried (Ed.), Internationales Management, Stuttgart 1981, pp. 1-44
Dülfer, Eberhard (Ed.), Personelle Aspekte im Internationalen Marketing , Berlin 1983
Dülfer, Eberhard, Die Auswirkungen der Internationaliserung auf Führung und Organisationsstruktur mittelständischer Unternehmen, in: BFuP, vol. 1985, no. 6, pp. 495-514
Dunn, Watson S., Effect of National Identity on Multinational Promotional Strategy in Europe, in: Jain, Subhash C., Tucker, Lewis R.jr., International Marketing: Managerial Perspectives, Boston/Mass.1979, pp.355-368
Dworak, Brigitte M., Das Länderrisiko als bankbetriebliches Problem, Berlin 1985
Ehrenfeld, Hildebert, Außenhandel, Direktinvestitionen und Lizenzen, Frankfurt/M., e.a.1975
Elliot ,William Y., Weltwirtschaft und Weltpolitik, Munich 1957
Engelhard, Werner Hans, Laßmann, Gert (Eds.), Anlagen-Marketing, in: ZfbF, vol. 1977, special supplement 7
Falkenhausen, Hasso Freiherr von, Organisation und Kontrolle in multinationalen Unternehmen, in: ZfbF, vol. 1975, special supplement 4, pp. 75-90
Feuerbach, Karl, Organisatorische Aspekte der Überwachung von Auslandsengagements, in: BFuP, vol. 1980, no. 3, pp. 229-247
Fieten, Robert, Financial Engineering - Komponente des industriellen Großanlagengeschäfts, in: Macharzina, Klaus (Ed.), Finanz- und bankwirtschaftliche Probleme bei internationaler Unternehmenstätigkeit, Stuttgart 1985, pp. 163-194
Gerber, Stephan, Risikoanalyse und Risikopolitik bei direkten deutschen Auslandsinvestitionen von mittelständischen Unternehmungen in Entwicklungsländern, Frankfurt/M. and Berne 1982
Graham, John L., Sano, Yoshihiro, Smart Bargaining - Doing Business with the Japanese, Cambridge/Mass. 1984
Graham, John L., Campbell, Nigel, Jolibert, Alain, Meissner, Hans Günther, A Comparision of Marketing Negotiations in France, Germany, the United Kingdom and the United States, Project Report, University of Southern California e.a. 1985
Günter, Bernd, Local Content - eine Herausforderung für das internationale Marketing in: Marketing, vol. 7, no. 4 (nov. 1985), pp. 263-274
Guldimann, Werner, Luftverkehr an der Jahrtausendwende, in: Neue Züricher Zeitung, no. 7 of 11.1.1983, p. 23

Gutenberg, Erich, Grundlagen der Betriebswirtschaftslehre, Vol. 2, Der Absatz, 17.Edn, Heidelberg e.a. 1984
Hahn, Dietger, Taylor, Bernhard (Eds.), Strategische Unternehemensplanung, 3 Edn., Würzburg, Vienna 1984
Hallen, Lars, Wiedersheim-Paul, Finn, Psychic Distance in International Marketing, Uppsala 1981 (Working Paper)
Hammann, Peter, Erichson, Bernd, Marktforschung, Stuttgart and New York 1978
Hellauer, Josef, Welthandelslehre, Wiesbaden 1950
Hielscher, Udo, Instrumente zur Begrenzung von Währungrisiken, in: BFuP, vol. 37, no. 6 (Nov,1985), pp. 531-548
Hill, Wilhelm, Marketing, in: Tietz, Bruno (Ed.) Handwörterbuch der Absatzwirtschaft, Stuttgart 1974, Sp. 1233-1247
Hinterhuber, Hans H., Strategische Unternehmungsführung, 3. Edn., Berlin and New York 1984
Höfner, Klaus, Eggle, Rainer, Internationales Management, in: Rationalisierung, vol. 33 (1982), no. 7/8, pp. 148-152
Holzmüller, Hartmut H., Grenzüberschreitende Konsumentenforschung, in: Marketing, vol. 8, no. 1 (feb 1986), pp.45-54
Institut der deutschen Wirtschaft (Eds.), Zahlen zur wirtschaftlichen Entwicklung der Bundesrepublik Deutschland 1986, Cologne 1986
Jahrreiß, Wolfgang, Zur Theorie der Direktinvestinvestitionen im Ausland, Berlin 1984
Kahn, Hermann, World Economic Development, New York 1979
Kebschull, Dietrich, Mayer, Otto G. (Eds.), Multinationale Unternehmen - Anfang oder Ende der Weltwirtschaft, Frankfurt/M. 1974
Kebschull, Dietrich, Ausländische Direktinvestitionen in Südostasien - ein internationaler Vergeich des Engagements in: Laumer, Helmut (Ed.), Wachstumsmarkt Südostasien, Munich, Cologne, London 1984, pp. 435-463
Keegan, Warren J., Multinational Marketing Management, Englewood Cliffs/N.J. 1974
Keegan, Warren J., MacMaster, Norman A., Global Strategic Marketing, in: Kirpalani, V.H. (Ed.) International Marketing, Chicago 1983, pp. 94-105
Kern, Werner, Zur Analyse des internationalen Transfers von Technologien, in: ZfbF, vol. 25, pp. 85-98
Kicherer, Hans Peter, Koordinationsaufgaben des Controllers im Bereich der Informationsversorgung internationaler Unternehmungen, in: Wacker, W.H., Haussmann, H., Kumar, B. (Eds.), Internationale Unternehmensführung, Berlin 1981, pp. 239-249
Klein, Heinrich J., Stationen zum Erfolg im größten Spezialglasmarkt der Welt, Lecture at the 39th conference of German Business Scientists on the 15th Oct. 1985 in Berlin
Kluckhohn, Clyde, Spiegel der Menschheit, Zürich 1951
Korean Overseas Information Service (Eds.), A Handbook of Korea, 4. Edn. , Seoul 1982
Kotler, Philip, Marketing of Management, 4th Edn., Englewood Cliffs/N.J. 1980
Kreikebaum, Hartmut, Strategische Unternehmensplanung, Stuttgart e.a. 1981
Kreikebaum, Hartmut, Personal- und kommunikationspolitische Aspekte der Unternehmensführung in Japan, in: Dülfer, Eberhard (Ed.), Personelle Aspekte im Internationalen Management, Berlin 1983, pp. 129-157
Krux, Max, Potthoff, Erich, Sieben, Günter (Eds.), Eugen Schmalenbach - der Mann, sein Werk, die Wirkung, Stuttgart 1984
Kuhn, Thomas, The Structure of Scientific Revolutions, 2nd Edn., Chicago 1970
Kulhavy, Ernest, Internationales Marketing, Linz 1981
Laumer, Helmut (Ed.), Wachstumsmarkt Südostasien, Munich, Colonge, London 1984
Leontiades, James, Multinational Corporate Strategy, Lexington/Mass., Toronto 1985
Levitt, Theodore, The Globalization of Markets, in: Havard Business Review, vol. 61, no. 3 (may 1983), pp. 92-102
Lewandowski, Rudolf, Prognose- und Informationssysteme, Berlin und New York 1974

Lück, Wolfgang, Trommsdorff, Volker (Eds.), Internationalisierung der Unternehmung, Berlin 1982
Lüder, Klaus, Strategische Standortplanung transnationaler industrieller Großunternehmen, in: Lück, Wolfgang, Trommsdorff, Volker (Eds.), Internationisierung der Unternehmung, Berlin 1982, pp. 415-438
Macharzina, Klaus (Ed.), Diskontinuitätenmanagement, Berlin 1984
Macharzina, Klaus, Strategische Fehlentscheidungen in der internationalen Unternehmung als Folge von Informationspathologien, in: Macharzina, Klaus (Ed.), Diskontinuitätenmanagement, Berlin 1984, pp. 77-140
Macharzina, Klaus, Welge, Martin (Eds.), Export und internationale Unternehmung, Stuttgart 1989
Majaro,Simon, International Marketing, London 1977
Malinowski, Bronislaw, Eine wissenschaftliche Theorie der Kultur, Zürich 1949
Markowitz, Harry M., Portfolio Selection, Efficient Diversification of Investments, New York 1959
Marr, Rainer, Problemaspekte bei der Entwicklung eines Wissenschaftsprogramms des "Internationalen Management" - aus personalwirtschaftlicher Sicht, in: Dülfer, Eberhard (Ed.), Personelle Aspekte im Internationalen Management, Berlin 1983, pp. 27-40
Meffert, Heribert (Ed.), Marketing im Wandel, Wiesbaden 1980, pp. 3-35
Meffert, Heribert, Althans, Jürgen, Internationales Marketing, Stuttgart 1982
Meffert, Heribert, Größere Flexibilität als Unternehmungskonzept, in: ZfbF, vol. 37, no. 2 (feb 1985), pp. 121-137
Meissner, Hans Günther, Anthropologische Grundlagen der Exportmarktforschung, Berlin 1959
Meissner, Hans Günther, Exportpolitik vom Standpunkt der Unternehmensführung, Herne and Berlin 1974
Meissner, Hans Günther, Joint Ventures, in: Büschgen, Hans E., e.a. (Eds.) Handwörterbuch der Finanzwissenschaft, Stuttgart 1976, 917-924
Meissner, Hans Günther, Entwicklungsperspektiven des internationalen Marketing: Zukünftige Szenarien und Meßprobleme, in: Meffert, H. (Ed.), Marketing im Wandel, Wiesbaden 1980, pp. 175-184
Meissner, Hans Günther, Außenhandels-Marketing, Stuttgart 1981
Meissner, Hans Günther, Sohn, Karl-Heinz (Eds.), Internationales Rohstoffmarketing, Dortmund 1981
Meissner, Hans Günther, Winkelgrund, Reinhard, Internationales Marketing als Herausforderung deutscher Unternehmen, in: Marketing, vol. 4, no. 2 (May 1982), pp. 115-121
Meissner, Hans Günther, Probleme der internationalalen Werbung im Überblick, in: Tietz, Bruno (Ed.), Die Werbung, vol. 3, Landsberg am Lech 1982, pp. 3018-3043
Meissner, Hans Günther, Aktuelle Fragen der Exportmarkt-erschließung, in: Mitteilungen der Bundesstelle für Außenhandelsinformation, April 1983
Meissner, Hans Günther, Garcia Echevarria, Santiago, Karenberg, Leutfried, Unternehmensführung in Schwellenländern, stat 229 der Schriftenreihe der Wissenschaftlichen Arbeitsgemeinschaft für Technik und Wirtschaft des Landes Nordrhein-Westfalen, Dortmund 1983
Meissner, Hans Günther, Marketing für Innovationen, in: Meissner, Hans Günther, Winkelgrund, Reinhard (Eds.), Marketing für Innovationen, Dortmund 1984, pp. 9-22
Meissner, Hans Günther, So erobern Sie schwierige Märkte, in: Rationalisierungs-Kuratorium der Deutschen Wirtschaft (Eds.), Export-Conference 1984, Düsseldorf 1984
Meissner, Hans Günther, Finanzierungskonditionen als Instrumente des Exportmarketing, in: Macharzina, Klaus (Ed.), Finanz- und bankwirtschaftliche Probleme bei internationaler Unternehmenstätigkeit, Stuttgart 1985, pp. 147-162
Meissner, Hans Günther, Japanische und deutsche Marketingstrategien: Ein struktureller Vergleich, in: Mitteilungen der Bundesstelle für Außenhandelsinformation, November 1985. [Engish version: Irish Marketing Review, Vol. I, Spring 1986, pp. 21–31]

Meissner, Hans Günther, Systemvergleich zwischen deutschen und japanischen Marktstrategien, in: Gaugler, Eduard, Meissner, Hans Günther, Thom, Norbert (Eds.), Zukunftsaspekte der anwendungsorientierten Betriebswirtschaftslehre, Stuttgart 1986, pp. 211-222

Meissner, Hans Günther, Singer, Hans, Jahn, Wolfgang, Banning, Thomas E., Die internationale Verschuldung als Problem der Unternehmensführung, vol. 237 of the series of publications of the wissenschaftlichen Arbeitsgemeinschaft für Technik und Wirtschaft des Landes Nordrhein-Westfalen, Dortmund 1985

Moser, Reinhard, Beschaffungs-, Absatz-,und Finanzierungsentscheidungen in ihrer internationalen Verflechtung, in: Lück, Wolfgang Trommsdorff, Volker (Eds.) Internationalisierung der Unternehmung als Problem der Betriebswirtschaftslehre, Berlin 1982, pp. 291-306

Müller, Stefan, Köglmayr, Hans-Georg, Die psychische Distanz zu Auslandsmärktem: Ein verkanntes Exporthemmnis, in: ZfbF, vol. 38, no. 9 (Sept. 1986), pp. 788-804

n. a., Informationen über die Märkte der Welt, in: Ernährungswirtschaft, no. 9, 1985, p. 33

n. a., Die Kapitalverflechtung der Unternehmen mit dem Ausland, in: Monthly Reports of the German Federal Bank, vol. 33, no. 10 (Oct. 1981), pp. 39

Neubaur, F.F., Das PIMS-Programm und Portfolio-Management, in Hahn, Dietger, Taylor, Bernard (Eds.) Strategische Unternehmungsplanung, 3rd Edn.1984, pp. 165-192

Ohling, Heiko, Export - Import - Spendition, 7th Edn., Wiesbaden 1973

Ohmae, Kenichi, Die Macht der Triade, Wiesbaden 1985

Pausenberger, Ehrenfried, Internationale Unternehmungen in Entwicklungsländern, Düsseldorf and Vienna 1980

Pausenberger, Ehrenfried, (Ed.), Internationales Management, Stuttgart 1981

Pausenberger, Ehrenfried, Finanzpolitik internationaler Unternehmungen: Notwendigkeit und Grenzen der Zentralisierung, in: Wacker, Wilhelm H., Haussmann, Helmut, Kumar, Brij (Eds.), Internationale Unternehmensführung Berlin 1981, pp. 177-190

Pausenberger, Ehrenfried, Völker, Harald, Praxis des internationalen Finanzmanagement: eine empirische Untersuchung von Finanzierung, Kapitalstrukturgestaltung und Cash Management in internationalen Unternehmen, Wiesbaden 1985

Pausenberger, Ehrenfried, Die Besetzung von Geschäftsführerpositionen in ausländischen Tochtergesellschaften, in: Dülfer, Eberhard (Ed.), Personelle Aspekte im Internationalen Management, Berlin 1983, pp. 41-59

Peebles, Dean M., Ryans, John K. jr., Vernon, Ivan R., Coordinating International Advertising, in : Jain, Subhash C., Trucker, Lewis R. jr. (Eds.), International Marketing: Managerial Perspectives, Boston/Mass. 1979, pp. 344-354

Perlitz, Manfred, Absatzorientierte Internationalisierungsstrategien, not published habilitation, Bochun 1979

Phatak, Arvind V., Managing Multinational Corporrations, New York, Washington, London 1974

Plettner, Bernhard, Zur Lage der europäischen Elektroindustrie, in: Siemens Zeitschrift, vol. 58, no. 2, 1984, pp. 5-10

Porter, Micheal E., Competetive Strategy, N. Y. 1980

Pümpin, Cuno, Management strategischer Erfolgspositionen, Berne and Stuttgart 1982

Raffée, Hans, Grundlagen und Ansätze des strategischen Marketing, in: Raffée, Hans, Wiedermann, Klaus-Peter (Eds.), Strategisches Marketing, Stuttgart 1985, pp. 5-9

Raffée, Hans, Segler, Kay, Marketingstrategien im Export, in : Dichtl, Erwin, Issing, Ottmar (Eds.), Exporte als Herausforderung für die deutsche Wirtschaft, Cologne 1984, pp. 277-307

Raffée, Hans, Marketing-Perspektiven der 80er Jahre, in: Marketing vol. 4, no. 2, pp. 1-16

Reichmann, Thomas, Controlling mit Kennzahlen, Munich 1985

Ringel, Karlrobert, Exportmarktforschung als Informationsaufgabe, Cologne amd Opladen 1963

Ringle, Günther, Exportmarketing, Wiesbaden 1977

Schmidt, Reinhard, Analyse der Länderverschuldung aus der Sicht der international tätigen Bank, in: Mazcharzina, Klaus (Ed.), Finanz- und betriebswirtschaftliche Probleme bei internationaler Unternehmenstätigkeit, Stuttgart 1985, pp. 47-73

Schnabel, Helmut, Investitionsfinanzierung in einem weltweit tätigen Unternehmen, in: ZfB, vol. 51, no. 12, pp. 1238-1245

Schneider, Dieter, Die Länderselektion als absatzstrategische Aufgabe exportorientierter mittelständischer Unternehmungen, in: Der Markt, vol. 95, pp. 69-78

Sheth, Jagdish N., A Conceptual Model of Long Range Multinational Marketing Planning, in: Managerial Perspectives, Boston/Mass. 1979, pp. 424-432

Sieber, Eugen, Die internationale Unternehmung, in: Engeleiter, Hans-Joachim (Ed.), Gegenwartsfragen der Unternehmensführung, Herne and Berlin 1966, pp. 51-68

Simon, Hermann, Eintrittsbarrieren und Eintrittsstrategien im japanischen Markt, in: ZfbF, vol. 37, no. 11 (Nov. 1985), pp. 943-955

Stahr, Günther, Auslandsmarketing, vol. 1, Marktanalyse, Stuttgart 1979

Stahr, Günther, Marktselektionsentscheidungen in Auslandsgeschäft, in: ZfbF, vol. 32, pp. 276-290

Statistisches Bundesamt (Ed.), Statistisches Jahrbuch 1985 für die Bundesrepublik Deutschland, Stuttgart and Mainz 1988

Steinmann, Horst, Kumar, Brij, Wasner, Albert, Die Internationaliserung von Mittelbetrieben, Wiesbaden 1977

Steinmann, Horst, Kumar, Brij, Internationalisierung von Mittelbetrieben - Mangementprobleme und Förderungsmöglichkeiten, in: BFuP, vol. 1985, no.6, pp. 515-530

Steffenhagen, Hartwig, Der Strategiebegriff in der Marketingplanung, Aachen ,Terpstra, Vern, International Marketing, 3 Edn., Chicago 1983

Tietz, Bruno, Die Werbedynamik der Konsumenten und Unternehmer in ihren Konsequenzen auf das Marketing,in: Marketing, vol. 4, no. 2, pp. 91-102

Tiewul, Sylvanus A.,The General and Political Principles of Behavior in the United Nations Code on Conduct of Transnational Corporations, in: Wacker, Wilhelm, Haussmann, Helmut, Kumar, Brij (Eds.), Internationale Unternehmensführung, Berlin 1981, pp.351-377

Tiong Tan, Chin, Sheth, Jagdish N. (Eds.), Historical Perspective in Consumer Research: Nation and International Perspectives, Proceedings of the Association for Consumer Research International Meeting in Singapore, july 18-20, 1985

Topritzhofer, Edgar, Moser, Reinhard, Das Exortgeschäft 2nd. Edn, Vienna 1984

Urban, Sabine, Réussir a l'exportation, Paris 1979

Vernon, Raymond, Future of the Multinational Enterprise, in: Kindleberger, Charles P. (Ed.), International Corporation, Cambridge/Mass., London 1970

Vogt, Victor, System der Exportförderung in der Bundesrepublik Deutschland, in: Stahr, Günter (Ed.), Exportpraxis - Handbuch für den deutschen Exporteur, A VIII

Wack, Pierre, Scenarios: Shooting the Rapids, in: Harvard Business Review, vol. 63, no.6 (Nov./Dec. 1985) pp. 139-150

Welge, Martin, Management in deutschen multinationalen Unternehmungen, Stuttgart 1980

Welge, Martin, Die Führung von Betriebseinheiten im Ausland aus organisatorischer Sicht, in : Dichtl, Erwin, Issing, Ottmar (Eds.), Exporte als Herausforderung für die deutsche Wirtschaft, Cologne 1984, pp. 369-395

Zahn, Ernest, Das unbekannte Holland, Berlin 1984

Zeira, Yoram, Banai, Moshe, Selection of Expatriate Managers in MNCs: The Host-Environment Point of View, in: International Studies of Man & Organisation, vol. XV, no. 1/1985

Zimmermann, Andreas, Spezifische Risiken des Auslandsgeschäfts, in: Dichtl, Erwin, Issing, Ottmar (Eds.), Exporte als Herausforderung für die deutsche Wirtschaft, Cologne 1984, pp. 105-139

Zünd, André, Kontrolle und Revision in der multinationalen Unternehmung, Bern 1971

Index of Subjects

MIX
Papier aus verantwortungsvollen Quellen
Paper from responsible sources
FSC® C105338

If you have any concerns about our products,
you can contact us on
ProductSafety@springernature.com

In case Publisher is established outside the EU,
the EU authorized representative is:
Springer Nature Customer Service Center GmbH
Europaplatz 3, 69115 Heidelberg, Germany

Printed by Libri Plureos GmbH
in Hamburg, Germany